Copyright (

Emerging Proud Press
The Enterprise Centre
Norwich NR4 7TJ
United Kingdom

ISBN: 978-1-9160860-0-5
www.EmergingProud.com

KindaPROUD
Stories of Hope & Transformation

DEDICATION

This book is dedicated to all those finding their way through the wilderness.

May you find your gifts, use them well, and shine unapologetically bright.

You are here to do amazing things.

"Our deepest fear is not that we are inadequate. Our deepest fear is that we are powerful beyond measure. It is our light, not our darkness that most frightens us."

Marianne Williamson

This project is dedicated to maintaining the integrity of the voices of the people that have shared their stories.

The stories shared are real life situations and some of them may contain language that could be triggering for some people, such as "overweight", "healthy weight", "obese", "weight-loss", and upsetting content. Some of the contributors express their experience firsthand of 'fat-phobic' behaviour. We recognise that each individual taking part in the project and reading this book will be at different stages of their transformation journey, and we want to honour that where we're all at is perfectly okay. If you are at all triggered by reading the stories, please seek support from the 'Resources' section in the back of the book.

The shocking truth is that, on a global level, 'fat-phobia' runs deep within our society. This is constantly being reinforced by the diet and health industry. We have been taught that weight = health, that weight = self-worth, and that our weight and our appearance hold a lot of importance with regards to our worthiness. This is a prejudice that we are attempting to tackle, and it's not easy and we may get it wrong at times. Something we acknowledge is that it's virtually impossible to publish a book like this and not cause offence to anyone; if you are triggered by reading any of the stories, please seek support from the resources in the back of the book. The antidote to this 'fat-phobic' and judgemental mindset is the Body Positive movement and the Health at Every Size © movement, which we support and feel aligned with.

The KindaProud pocket books are a wonderful resource, full of amazing stories of transformation. I was deeply moved and inspired by reading them.

Dr Steve Taylor, Author and Lecturer

Contents

Praise for this KindaProud
Pocket Book

#Emerging Proud through Disordered Eating, Body Image and Low Self-Esteem is a powerful book sharing inspiring recovery stories; stories that echo and validate some of my own deep journey through the dark night of the soul of chronic illness and spiritual crisis, to deeper levels of health, light and freedom. Thank you all for sharing your stories and inspiring others on what is possible no matter how dark it gets. We all have a vast potential for awakening to our true essence, and often it's that darkness that initiates us into our true self, stories such as these need to be told and heard widely.

Frances Goodall, Founder of the Women's Wellness Circle www.womenswellnesscircle.com and www.francesgoodall.com

If you want to help someone find their way, tell a story. KindaProud has taken that old adage to heart by sharing stories of individuals who have taken many different paths to find their true selves – and in doing so, discovered a life beyond their wildest dreams. These are tales of transformation, offering hope and inspiration to anyone seeking freedom from eating difficulties and body image distress.

Anita Johnston. Ph.D.
Author, Eating in the Light of the Moon,
Light of the Moon Cafe
www.DrAnitaJohnston.com

Transformative, beautiful, and completely sums up what it means to 'emerge proud'.

Stevie Grice-hart, Body Positivity Activist and lgbtqia @bopo.boy on Twitter

A beautifully honest and inspiring support for anyone who'd like a kinder relationship with their body. May the words of these shining, powerful souls inspire you to celebrate yourself exactly as you are.

Ellie Paskell, An energetically awakened woman and Somatic Soul Coach who supports others to follow the wisdom in their bodies to revolutionise their lives. www.elliepaskell.com

Empowering, inspirational and life-affirming is this honest collection of heartfelt transformation stories. Read proud, feel proud and be proud

Michael Brown, Author of Mercurial
www.poetbrownie.com

Resilience

When I think I've reached the end
More problems onto me descend
The only thing that I can do
Is find a way to get me through

Each day I take one at a time
The only way this hill to climb
Not dwelling on all that is wrong
But dealing with and moving on

By each hurdle I overcome
I see how far from hell I've come
As staying put does me no good
So ploughing on I can and should

— Ambriel

About KindaProud

Our KindaProud Pocket Book series
Ethos and Message

Why do we need 'KindaProud' Pocket Books of Hope and Transformation? There is a rising epidemic of mental health problems in our society, and alongside it a pervasive negative prognosis message that goes out to those who are struggling emotionally. It's our shared belief, due to our personal experiences, that one of the most important elements of getting back on a road to recovery (and ultimately transformation) is to normalise these experiences and to hear personal stories of HOPE from those who have been there before and not just survived, but thrived.

Each Pocket Book has its own KindaProud Rep; a Peer who has personal experience of 'coming through' the theme of that specific book. These are the first 4 books currently in the series: -

- #Emerging Proud through NOTEs (Non-Ordinary Transcendent Experiences)

- #Emerging Proud through Disordered Eating, Poor Body Image and Low Self- Esteem

- #Emerging Proud through Suicide

- #Emerging Proud through Trauma and Abuse

What are the main Aims and Objectives of the KindaProud Pocket Book series?

- To relieve people of the distress associated with transformational crises by offering authentic examples of personal stories and resources to engender hope and initiate recovery.

- To decrease stigma, improve wellbeing and influence the saving of lives by providing a more compassionate and positive conceptual framework for emotional distress.

- To use the profits from book sales to continue to distribute free books, and hence messages of HOPE, to mental health facilities, and those in need, all around the world.

All of the stories in this book have been kindly donated by Peers who have personally experienced this specific theme of distress and 'emerged transformed'; dedicated to giving hope that there is light at the end of the tunnel to others who may still be suffering. This book series is totally not-for-profit, was seed-funded by *The Missing Kind charity* and continues to be supported voluntarily through the endless dedication of each Peer Rep., our Ambassador and Publisher Sean Patrick of *That Guy's House* who supported us to set up #Emerging Proud Press, and Jenna Gould, our 'PR Guru' of *Media Jems*.

Meet Sean our Publisher and Ambassador!

I guess you could say that I was a typical Millennial/Gen Y kind of guy. I lived life on the 'ordinary' path; going from High School to College to University to my first job in the City. Embracing all of the joys of young professional city life (like I'd seen so much on TV growing up), however, having the curse of also knowing that my life needed to have meaning and without it I was doomed. And so, right on time, feelings of anxiety and depression became present in my early 20s, with social anxiety leading on to more serious depression.

Like many people I didn't know where I fitted into the

world, and despite having the things I was 'supposed to', I felt unhappy, anxious and unfulfilled. I felt like I was on a treadmill and scared by the world.

My 'crisis point' hit when I started to experience severe panic attacks at 22 years old. It was then that I had no option but to admit I had problems that at that time I couldn't rationalise with my own intellect or understanding. In other words, I was having a mental health crisis.

I started by reading books, gaining a better understanding of my own mind, and ultimately to a more spiritual outlook on life through daily meditation and adopting spiritual beliefs. I had read these books from being 15 so it was 'old hat' for me, however, a 22-year-old having a crisis could engage with them with much more desperation than a 15-year-old wanting to be *his best self.*

After accepting an expat job in Hong Kong and spending half a year away from my 'ordinary life', I had the chance to recalibrate, explore meditation and mindfulness, and let go of damaging old patterns and beliefs.

I turned my life upside down.

On returning home, I set up a blog called *That Guy Who Loves The Universe* and began to share ideas about spirituality and positive mental health with my following, which grew to over 15,000 people. I began to speak at conferences and wellness events all over the world and released an Amazon bestseller in July 2016. My mess latterly became my message.

In 2017, I developed my own wellness company, *That Guy's House*, with a main focus on wellness books and mental health projects.

After meeting Katie, the project's Founder, via a synchronistic introduction by our *#Emerging Proud through Suicide* book Rep., Kelly, and finding out more about the #Emerging Proud campaign, Katie and I both knew that bringing our personal experiences and skills together to launch the KindaProud series of Pocket Books would be the perfect collaboration.

Meet the Project's Founder

My name is Katie Mottram and I'm the Founder of the #Emerging Proud campaign, through which the KindaProud book series has been birthed. #Emerging Proud is a grassroots social movement aimed at: 'Re-framing mental distress as a catalyst for positive transformation'; providing a platform for people who have 'emerged transformed' through a personal crisis and feel called to share their story and give hope to others. By no means does this mean the end of our personal journey, but rather that we now choose to view life's challenges more as growth opportunities as opposed to experiences set out to destroy us.

I was called to start this movement due to finding that re-framing my own crisis as a transformational growth process (which still continues!), and hearing the experiences of others, was the thing that helped me to connect with my authentic Self and start to live the life I was born to live.

When I experienced a personal crisis in 2008, what I needed was to know that I wasn't alone in my experiences, that what I was going through was 'normal', and a message of HOPE, that all would be okay, not that there was anything 'wrong' with me. I needed to connect with others who had been through similar challenges and were able to walk alongside me whilst I found my own way out of the darkness.

In the last decade, it has been through my own research; looking at more empowering ways of understanding what happened to me, my reactions to it, and how to go about self-healing, in addition to connecting with my amazing peers and listening to their stories, that has really set me on my own path of healing. This feels like the complete opposite of what I had been told was helpful whilst working within mental health services for 15 years previously. Hence my passion to provide others with some of the tools that helped me not only to survive, but to thrive and love life.

You can read my full story in my own book, *Mend the Gap: A transformative journey from deep despair to spiritual awakening*, which was published in 2014.

I truly hope that this book, and the others in the 'Pocket Books of Hope and Transformation' series, inspires and supports you in your own evolutionary journey...

And, remember: let that light you hold deep inside shine unapologetically bright!

Find out more about the campaign and what we're up to at: **www.emergingproud.com**

Meet our Peer Pocket Book Rep
- Amy Woods

Amy Woods is Kinda Proud, and so she should be! She's emerged through years of self-criticism transformed, to give hope and support to others who are still struggling. We couldn't be prouder to have Amy as one of our KindaProud Pocket Books of Hope and Transformation Reps! Here's Amy's story...

"What if the journey isn't about becoming anything, what if it's about UN-becoming everything that isn't you so you could be who you were meant to be in the first place."
— Paolo Coelho

I remember the feeling well....It was like a black hole of never being satisfied and obsessing about my next mouthful of food. I fantasised about what I would eat next, what I'd get from the shops to devour later and how I would hide it. The shame, the secrecy, the manipulation of urgently needing to eat so badly! Just eat and eat and eat...

I remember having a meal with some friends and family members when I was about 18, reaching for portion number three when someone shouted: 'Amy, stop eating! You'll get fat if you keep eating'. I was completely taken by surprise and to my horror realised that I'd been caught out. From this place of utter embarrassment, I tried to defend myself to deflect the hurt when they responded: 'Well, you're putting on weight...'

In that moment, the long-tunnel-vision, punch-in-the-stomach, red-cheek-flare of shame washed over my body like a heavy wave of absolute failure. Something within me cracked open. From this place of shame, embarrassment, humiliation and deep hurt, a door that was holding back so much emotion flung wide open. I cried all night and 2 days after that. The utter heartbreak I felt was unbearable and tears kept coming, and coming. Until I eventually found some peace. I felt cleansed, light and liberated. I realised that for so long, for years, I had actually numbed myself of feeling any kind of emotion and had imprisoned myself in a box of self-judgement and self-criticism. I realised that for a very long time I had been completely rejecting my body, hating it even; feeling frustrated every time I looked in the mirror and saw my hideous self looking back at me.

The encounter had completely cracked me open and, for the first time in what seemed like forever, I felt an aliveness, a peace and a connection to something so much bigger than me. Around the same time I had started to come across authors such as Marianne Williamson and Eckhart Tolle, where they explained much of what I was feeling and opened my eyes to this 'other world' where all beings are connected in the source or the Oneness. This was the beginning of a long journey of UN-becoming everything that wasn't me and embracing everything that was me.

A few months later I came across the Institute for the Psychology of Eating. They were talking about how the relationship we have with our food is ultimately a reflection of the relationship we have with life. When I came across their ethos, I started to understand that my binge eating was a result of years and years of not knowing how to process the intense emotions I was feeling: it was a result of DIS-connection from my soul and from the Oneness of life, it was a result of not feeling able to express who I was and what I wanted, it was the result of being so severely disconnected from my Wildish nature and the natural world around me.

It was an intense way of my body and my soul desperately trying to get my attention.

"DIS-ordered eating is the body's way of coping

with a DIS-ordered world"
—Marc David, Founder of the
Institute for the Psychology of Eating

I started to discover that there was so much more to the story than me being a weak failure with a complete lack of willpower. I started to become aware of the tremendously judgemental and critical narrative I lived my life through and actually realised I had a choice, and the willingness to transform it into something positive.

I then went on to discover books like *The Gifts of Our Compulsions*, by Mary O'Malley, *Women Who Run With the Wolves*, by Clarissa Pinkola Estes and *Body Positive Power*, by Megan Crabbe, and learned more and more about where this mentality of self-blaming and shaming comes from and why we have different self-sabotaging behaviours. All of this opened my eyes to the fact that we are so much more than our physical appearance. We are spiritual beings living an imperfect and emotional human experience with a purpose. We are each here for a reason; we belong to Mother Earth, and the realisation that we are unconditionally accepted and loved by her helped me begin to heal my relationship with my body and my food.

Understanding that it was ok to feel EVERYTHING from the heartache to the ecstasy and everything in between.

Understanding that the voices that were telling me

I was not flawless enough, thin enough or beautiful enough, are not who I truly am and knowing that they are ghosts of a narrative so deeply ingrained within our collective consciousness that we inherit them on a subconscious level from the human world around us.

The transformation I experienced through starting to heal my binge eating and my unhealthy body image inspired me to train as an Eating Psychology Coach and support and empower others to feel free, alive and worthy.

By no means is my binge eating eradicated completely, nor is my life a self-rejecting-free party. It's a life-long journey of recovery and some days it's easier than others to be kind and compassionate to myself. But it's safe to say that, most of the time, I am no longer afraid to be myself, to speak my truth and fight for what I believe in.

If you are reading this and are struggling with your relationship to food, your body image or low self-esteem, please know that it does get easier, things will change. You are strong, you are so strong actually, hang on in there and reach out for support in any way you can. I believe in you. You are worthy, you are resilient and you are so flipping beautiful.

Doing this with the support and love of people who understand and have been through similar things has made this journey a lot easier and so much more fun too. I am so grateful for meeting people like Katie who are doing such inspiring things to bring hope to so many people who are struggling in a world that tells them there is something 'wrong'.

There is nothing wrong. This is your time for transformation. Love, Amy x

Amy Woods is a Certified Eating Psychology Coach and Reiki Drum Practitioner, specialising in Compulsive Eating, cultivating a healthy body image culture and empowering people to transform the relationship with the food they eat and the body they're in from one of shame and guilt to one of nourishment and pleasure.

She is Founder and Director of the social enterprise SoulShine, which aims to empower people of all ages to live their fullest and most authentic lives. Through the means of coaching sessions, workshops, talks, support groups, online courses and body positive photo shoots, SoulShine aims to build a supportive and compassionate Body Positive Community where each person is celebrated for who they are.

Amy is highly motivated and passionate about creating positive change within her community and believes that it is OK to be who you are, that you are MORE than enough already, that the world needs your gifts and you are worthy of living a fucking amazing life!

Come and join the Body Positive Revolution!

Find out more information at:
www.soul-shine.org.uk

Mel is Kinda Proud of how she travelled beyond her negative self-image to set herself free

Mel discovered that the answer to her healing took a brave leap of faith to do something outside of her comfort zone, only then did she discover that she was capable of everything she'd previously told herself she couldn't do. We think she's a 'f**king soldier' for overcoming her limiting beliefs too!

When I was a kid I loved Kylie Minogue and Jason Donovan. Neighbours was one of my favourite TV shows and I really, really wanted to go to Australia. I thought it sounded like the coolest place in the world, but my family told me it was very far away and very expensive to get to. We mostly went on holiday to Butlins which, if you've never had the pleasure of going, involves hyperactive kids and incredibly drunk parents. I knew there wasn't much hope of ever getting to Australia.

Nobody I knew in my hometown in the Midlands, UK ever went travelling. Gap years were for rich kids. Backpacking was for sporty types who wanted to go trekking and kayaking. I hated sport. I got laughed at for coming last in cross-country at school. I hated PE lessons because we had to wear gym shorts and I hated my thighs. On holiday, I was even embarrassed to wear a swimming costume in front of my family - I wore a big baggy t-shirt over it whenever possible.

When I was in my early twenties, a friend from my hometown announced, quite suddenly, that he was going to travel around the world. This friend was like me, working in a minimum wage job in hospitality, and he referred to our town as the 'black hole of dreams'. I'd already tried to go to university and dropped out. My confidence was low and my anxiety was at an all-time high.

My friend travelled around the world for about ten months. He sent me emails telling me about all the people he'd met and all the awesome stuff he was doing. His family weren't rich - he'd saved up all that money himself. I'd told myself for so long that I was too poor, too fat and not sporty enough to do anything like that; my excuses were proving weak. But, there was the whole swimsuit problem...

My first swimming lesson at primary school did not go well. We each had to get in the pool so the teacher could see our swimming ability. I was so scared that I couldn't get my arms and legs to work. I felt myself sinking, literally and metaphorically, as the entire class laughed. I was bullied a lot at primary school for being the weird, fat, poor kid with divorced parents, but I was also teased by adults outside of school too. It's taken a lot of therapy to work through the pain of constantly feeling ashamed of myself.

My friend came back from his travels. He kept telling me 'if I can do it, you can'. A female friend at work was planning to go to Australia. Seeing another woman plan a trip alone was the final push I needed. It took years of saving up money, but eventually I bought a working holiday visa for Australia. I lost myself in the logistics, until the day I booked flights. That's when sh*t got real.

How was I going to survive so far away from my family? What the hell was I going to wear on the beach? I looked at those frilly dress-style swimming costumes that bigger women are expected to wear. Why should we have to wear horrible frumpy things, or be expected to cover up, just to make other people feel more comfortable? So I bought a tankini - a halter top and bottoms. It felt nicer than a swimming costume, but it wasn't as scary as a bikini. I still wasn't sure I'd be able to wear it in public. In the few weeks before my flight, with help from friends and my parents, I continually countered my inner critical voice. I didn't refer to it as that back then - I thought it was normal to have those kind of negative thoughts. My inner critic told me I was going to fail. That I'd run home to my parents again and get laughed at.

Just before I left, my friend gave me a pep talk. He said if I ever doubted myself I should look in the mirror and say 'I'm a f**king soldier'. I told him that was f**king stupid. He kept saying, 'mate, you've just gotta do it - tell yourself, I'm a f**king soldier'. So, I was in the toilets at Heathrow airport, my stomach in knots, sitting on the loo, saying over and over in my head, 'I'm a f**king soldier'. I didn't care if it was stupid at that point, I had to try it.

I thought I'd probably just spend a few months in Australia and then miss home and come back. I ended up travelling for over five years.

Going travelling is often seen as a form of escapism, and that's okay. Sometimes you need to get out of the town you grew up in so you can start to heal. I met people from all over the world and my confidence grew. I continually proved myself wrong and did things that I never thought short fat girls from the Midlands were allowed to do. I wore my tankini on the beach every bloody day, because getting on that plane was the scariest thing I ever did and I was

21

damned if I was going to let swimwear defeat me.

On reflection, maybe it wasn't about swimwear after all. I channelled all my anxieties into my body in the hope that I could change it. If I just lost weight it would solve everything. When really, it was a childhood of being told I was never good enough and constantly being asked to change myself. Through all my different travels, living a life of swimming in the sea every day and eating all different kind of foods, I never lost weight. I spent four months in India and got very sick. I barely ate for weeks, and I still wasn't thin. It was at that point I made the promise to myself that I would never try to force my body into a different size or shape. All that matters is my health and that I have a healthy relationship with food with no rules, no dieting, no restrictions. It doesn't matter what size I am – it's my mental and physical health that matters. I will never be thin, and that's fine. I am no longer afraid of being fat. There are so many worse things to be than fat.

Learning to be more comfortable in swimwear was just the side effect. What I learnt was a wider perspective, whilst unlearning all the rules I grew up with. It's a long journey of self-love, but I'm pleased to be learning about the world and myself, and I hope to now be able to help others who've been through similar things. I work for an eating disorder charity and I'm training to be a counsellor. Everyone deserves to feel good about themselves, irrelevant of where they come from or what they look like. But it starts with doing something scary - pushing yourself out of your comfort zone. It's worth the leap of faith, I promise.

Mel

Keep up with Mel's inspiring blogs via these social media platforms:

Twitter: @MCiavucco

IG: @MelCiavucco

FB page: The Compassionate Feminist

www.melciavucco.weebly.com

It took finding Peers who accepted her for her authentic Self, to enable Fran from Australia to be brave enough to love herSelf for who she truly is...plus lots of coffee!

We couldn't agree more with Fran, when she says:

'When social judgement and expectations conflict with the call to authenticity, the result is suffering.'

We love Fran's inspiring story, and we hope that you find some inspiration in it to be Kinda Proud of your-Self too...

24

My journey as a transgender woman really began at age 15, when I realised that my adult sexual identity did not match my body or the social identity I had grown up with. I grew up in a tiny, and very conservative, rural community - bitterly divided by racial trauma and the history of colonisation. I experienced bullying, domestic violence and neglect as a child. I was very anxious growing up. I would escape into fantasy and imagination. I didn't feel secure or loved for being myself.

My first instinct was to hide. I couldn't tell anyone. I struggled with my feelings and identity alone. I had internalised so much stigma and blame and fear from those around me that I could not accept or care for myself. I split into two people as the only way I could handle having different feelings and identities that could not be reconciled. I had an internal identity and an external identity, they were distinct, they had different genders.

Gender and sexuality come from within, and are far more diverse and complex than traditionally understood. When social judgement and expectations conflict with the call to authenticity the result is suffering.

I lived this way for 20 years, experiencing bouts of sadness and lethargy, losing jobs, drifting from place to place. I didn't seek help. I didn't understand why I felt unhappy most of the time. I felt stuck, blocked, unable to make authentic relationships, unable to be an adult, or a real person, at all. It was like I didn't exist.

I was unhappy with my body. I hated to look at myself in the mirror. It wasn't how I thought of myself, inside. I had terrible acne which didn't help at all. I got very overweight. I felt shame and loathing. I lived online, creating female identities and roleplaying. I got very addicted to a virtual existence which gave me things I didn't think I could have in real life. Things drifted out of control.

Eventually I was diagnosed with depression. I couldn't work. I was tired all of the time. I started medication but nothing seemed to help. I started the long process of coming out. My family were not very accepting. I felt I had to move interstate to a place I could get help and be myself. It was disastrous, cutting myself off from everyone I knew. I got very unwell.

Gender transition was very, very hard. I experienced housing and employment discrimination, street harassment, social anxiety and paranoia. All at a time when I was at my lowest ebb; when my mental, emotional, social and financial resources were stretched beyond breaking point.

Medical supports were not very helpful. The gender clinic psychiatrist said my mental distress was something other trans women did not have, and it meant I was not suitable for gender reassignment. My peers advised me to lie. I refused. Saying that I didn't want gender reassignment was the only way I could take back control of my own life and identity.

Saying it made it true - for a long while. I got very angry.

My LGBT-specific GP was very good. He was my only real medical support for a long time and never stopped trying to help me. But his office was a long way across town. I was too frightened and tired to risk going to a doctor who didn't understand being trans – it's not something you want to explain every time you visit a clinic with a cold. There were many times when I was too sick to get to my doctor. Living alone without any support is very hard.

I trace my recovery journey from discovering peer support groups. Peer support was there for me when I couldn't afford professional help, when the volunteer counsellor said she didn't understand what words meant when I used them. In peer support I felt that I'd found my crowd - we were all crazy but I was no crazier than anyone else.

Around this time I was diagnosed with type II diabetes. I went on medication, I tested my blood sugar daily. It was a struggle to take care of myself - sometimes I failed and things got out of control. Balancing physical illness and medication while struggling with depression on my own was very difficult.

Eventually I began volunteering and facilitating a support group. I got a job answering the phones at the support group charity head office. One day I noticed I was no longer the most unwell person in the room. I was surprised.

I had been to a psychiatrist and been given a diagnosis of Borderline Personality Disorder. I rejected it angrily, I was convinced it would prevent me from ever getting gender reassignment. I refused to go back... but I felt ambivalent about my rejection. What if he was right? It seemed like a way forward. Eventually I went back.

I started working on mindfulness. Being aware of what I was thinking and feeling. Putting a mindful pause between what happened to me and my reaction to it. Being able to observe myself, my thoughts and feelings. I began working on self care; my physical, financial and emotional needs. I fought back with exercise and diet. I got my blood sugar under control and went off the diabetes medication.

The psych meds weren't helping me any more and I had been too mentally disorganised to take them regularly, which was disastrous for my mood and functioning. I slowly weaned off them. A key point came when my psychiatrist said that my distress was not caused by a chemical imbalance in my head. This rocked me back on my heels some. If my problem wasn't bio-chemical in nature then why was I taking the pills at all? With support from my psychiatrist and mental health nurse, and using coping skills and breathing techniques, and exercise and sleep hygiene I slowly weaned off the remaining pills.

The only medications I use now are hormones and

the occasional sleeping medication. Good sleep is important. I don't reject medication completely. I think my mental health nurse said it best: you do whatever it takes to help you stay sane.

I call mine a coffee-led recovery. When I was unwell and unemployed one of the hardest things was not being able to afford a cup of coffee. Being able to sit down, warm your hands, drink a cup of tea or coffee and relax and reflect on your day is refreshing and energising. It's especially important when you're feeling tired and unwell, and when you're a long way from home and travelling by foot or public transport. Have you noticed how few warm places there are to sit down in our modern world if you have no money? I recommend public libraries.

These days I send out texts to all my friends on the weekend offering to meet for coffee. Someone always wants to! I'll always offer to pay and let them get the next one. I don't care when the next one is, I'm not counting. I try to live by my values and my values are friendship and coffee. It's no surprise that I'm a well-known regular at my favourite cafes.

People often talk about saving money in terms of giving up the cup of coffee. I look at it differently. Small pleasures make life happier, and when you're happy you're less likely to impulse spend or make mistakes. Coffee is one of the last things I'd give up to save money.

I had always loved to draw since I was a small child.

Growing up I learned to draw people and I became obsessed with drawing portraits. Through university and work I got through lectures and meetings drawing people, sketching and doodling. When I was unwell my drawing ebbed away to almost nothing. I saw a poster for a life drawing class in a local shop and went along. I found another community I could belong to, a new identity as an artist. I made new friends, a new identity.

Drawing nudes, both male and female, was a revelation of the beauty and honesty of the human form. I felt connected to something. Life models are wonderful, beautiful people. It is a privilege to draw them. I began to wonder if I could model one day. What would people see if they drew my body? Would my body ever reflect who I am inside? Could I overcome my fear of being seen, or being intimate in that way?

I became a peer support worker. I trained, I began working with people in crisis. I began to learn more about mental health, about what it takes to become well. I started to look at my own life and wonder if I dared to admit what I wanted, if I dared to become well, if I dared to become whole. I was challenged by changing attitudes. If my friends could accept me, if my community could accept me, why couldn't I learn to accept myself?

Gender dysphoria - the unhappiness of having an inner identity different to my outward gender - made me feel blocked from many things. I felt frightened and incapable of intimacy or relationships. A friend asked me to go to an LGBT partner slow dance. I was frightened, but I wanted to. I had started to realise that acceptance comes from within – it's about my heart, not about my body. I love dancing, being held, communicating through touch, feeling cared for. I wanted more.

I had some money, I saved more. I gave up having a car. I was disciplined. I knew what I wanted and I was prepared to be honest with myself. I had gender reassignment surgery last year. It was much harder physically than I had expected: weeks of pain, weakness and recovery. I'd always been a robust, basically healthy and resilient person, so I thought I would recover quickly. Instead I endured. Anxiety made it worse, and made the pain harder to bear, but I survived.

I feel more at home with my body. It's not perfect but I have no regrets. I did a life modelling workshop and learned the skills of being a model. I have modelled for my own community life drawing group, my own friends. I have seen the art people make from looking at my nude body. It helps me to feel good about myself. Being accepted by others helps me to accept myself. Having friends helps me be compassionate to myself.

As illustrations of this story I have included some drawings of me by a friend in my life drawing group.

This year I have become obsessed with dancing.

I have found joy in moving to rhythm and music. I've found connection and intimacy – romance – in dancing with a partner. I love to dance Lindy Hop and Charleston to swing jazz music. I learned to dance both roles, lead and follow. Dancing is so emotional, so blissful, so frustrating, so frightening. I love to be held. I love the way my body moves. I love the way my body feels. I love to dance. Something has unlocked. I remember when I was very young that I wanted to dance. I wanted to be a ballerina. Dancing is coming home. I dream about dancing sometimes. Through dancing, drawing and modelling I have found myself.

I think over the last 12 months I've tended to identify as practically asexual; more interested in romance and physical closeness than sex. That may change as time passes, or it may not. In one sense I'm nearly 50 years old, in another a little over 1. In a sense I think I've been about 15 for a long time. What I have mostly works well for now. Your horizon shrinks when you are in pain and distress, my horizon is now pushing out a little. I'm trying to learn to relax about it all.

In 2018 I participated in a scientific study that found some genetic influences on transgender identity in trans women. The week I started to write this I was running all over town being interviewed by newspapers and TV about what it feels like to be transgender and what this discovery means for people. I hope perhaps understanding of possible biological causes will lead to greater acceptance, particularly from family. Rejection by family is one of the most painful aspects of LGBT experience. Greater acceptance is already happening. In 2018 here in Australia the community spoke decisively in favour of equal marriage. This year people are saying children and teachers deserve protection from discrimination on the basis of gender and sexuality at school. A key milestone in my experience was being challenged by greater community acceptance to start to find a way to accept myself. Your acceptance, your compassion matters – especially to those in your own family and community.

I hope that my story helps you to find yourself, to accept yourself, to learn how to care for yourself, to find your way home. Never give up hope.

Rachel's work helped her to really see the truth

'Everybody's body is different, unique – and beautiful. There is no such thing as the "perfect" body'

We are Kinda Proud of Photographer Rachel from Norwich, UK, for sharing her experience of coming through breast cancer and bravely getting in front of the camera...

'I soon realised that the main fear I had – that everyone else is totally confident in their perfect bodies – was completely unfounded'...

When Amy Woods of SoulShine asked me to take photos at the first Wild Woman Photoshoot, my initial reaction was 'yes!', followed by a small amount of apprehension. I thought it was an absolutely brilliant thing – empowering women to represent themselves as they want to be represented, promoting body positivity, celebrating ourselves and our bodies as they are, encouraging self-acceptance and boosting self-esteem. But, as someone who has my own particular body confidence issues, I wasn't sure how it was going to make me feel.

I was diagnosed with breast cancer in 2014, at the age of 31. Since then I have had a mastectomy (and opted not to have reconstruction), and have gained over 2 stone in weight due to ongoing medication. So whilst I was fully on board with what Amy and Soulshine were doing, and very happy to take the photos, there was a small part of me that thought it might make me feel a bit sad; that here were all these women with their beautiful, whole, perfect bodies, and I'd never have the confidence to be so free and comfortable in my own skin, and get in front of the camera like they were.

But...

Within a very short time of arriving at the first photo shoot, I realised the reality was so far from those doubts and fears that I'd had. Amy and the SoulShine team held the space so beautifully, and I quickly felt very much at ease. I soon realised that the main fear I had – that everyone else is totally confident in their perfect bodies – was completely unfounded. As I photographed women of different shapes, sizes and ages, I started to really see the truth – everybody's body is different, unique – and beautiful. There is no such thing as the 'perfect' body. It's a myth created by society, the media, whoever. Seeing these women gradually increase in confidence and become more comfortable in themselves throughout the day was really empowering, so much so that by the end of the shoot I was starting to think 'I could do that – I could get in front of the camera next time!'

The next time came around, and again Amy asked me to be the photographer for the day. I had at the back of my mind that maybe I'd ask someone to take some photos of me at some point, but I wasn't sure. It was a bigger group than before, and I didn't know everyone...but I shared a little of my experience at the start of the day, and immediately felt heard and accepted. And again, as the day went on and the SoulShine team skilfully led us through exercises to help us connect to our true selves, to let go of the things that are holding us back, the 'shame gremlins' that stop us from achieving all we're capable of by telling us we're not good enough/pretty enough/thin enough/etc., I felt it again. That feeling that 'I could do that'.

And so when I tentatively suggested that maybe I could be in some of the photos, it was welcomed with open arms (literally – I've never known a group hug like it!).

Before I knew it I was wearing just a sarong, standing shoulder-to-shoulder with a group of friends, some of whom had been complete strangers just hours before, with a camera pointing at us – and I didn't feel self conscious at all. All that shame about how my body looks now just dropped away, with that realisation resounding in my heart – our bodies are all different, all unique – and all beautiful.

Amy says: 'The Wild Woman Photo Shoot is an opportunity for anyone who identifies as a woman to celebrate themselves and their body. What we [SoulShine] offer is a safe, supportive and compassionate space for women to express, embrace and celebrate their truest selves. It is a day of empowerment and 're-wilding' in beautiful surroundings with sisters.

In ceremony and through meditation, singing, dancing, drumming and of course eating. With playful souls and open hearts, we offer you a non-judgemental, compassionate, loving and supportive space to embrace your body, celebrate who you are and awaken the Wild Woman within. Whether you wish to show your Warrior, Wild Woman, your inner Goddess or your inner pixie, we will support you every step of the way to feel confident and proud of who you are. We want to prove that it doesn't matter what shape or size you are, moments of deep empowerment and true beauty are able to shine when we are able to drop all our limiting beliefs and the shame we carry around with us all the time. This is a time to say goodbye to that little voice that says: "you're not x enough, you're too x, you can't possibly have your photo taken!"'

"Within every woman there is a wild and natural creature, a powerful force, filled with good instincts, passionate creativity and ageless knowing, her name is Wild Woman but she is an endangered species."

—Clarissa Pinkola Estes

Serena from Norfolk tells us how it took coming close to death to 'Emerge' as a new woman

It's hearing real-life raw personal stories that can create change in someone's life: KindaProud Pocket Books of Hope and Transformation aim to create a positive domino effect, where more and more people like Serena can stand tall and speak out in order to give their Peers permission to do the same. Thank you for your bravery and inspiration Serena, we're very proud to have you appear in our KindaProud book...

Stepping Out of the Shower into my New Life

I planned to start writing this like all good stories begin – from the start – however I feel the need to lay down bare the impact that my journey of starving and exercise addiction had on me in the first instance.

On a sunny day in the late Summer of 2008 I desperately needed a shower as I had just been for a 5 mile run in the midday heat, after spending 2 hours on the exercise bike, and having not eaten in 3 days. My last meal had been my standard handful of Cheerios and quarter of a tin of tuna, and it was safe to say that my body was exhausted.

As I ran the shower I undressed in front of my full-length mirror, and as I did I felt that feeling of absolute disgust; to the extreme that I had to look away after a few minutes to stop myself from bursting into tears.

I climbed into the floor-to-ceiling shower cubicle and began to wash my hair, tepid water bouncing off my overheated skin. As I worked my way down, washing my neck, chest and stomach, my hands knocked into each protruding bone, and glided over muscles that ached from not being allowed to rest.

What happened next caused an absolute 360 degrees turn-around in my life.

As I woke with confusion and blurred vision, I realised that I was immersed in warm water and

I could taste soap in my mouth. The air was close and moist, and I was struggling to breathe from the heavy steam that was laying on my chest.

With my body feeling weak, I managed to use my slender arms to prop myself up against the white tiled wall, so I was slumped over like a tired rag doll. I used one hand and foot to pull the glass door of the cubicle back and let out a sigh of relief while taking a huge breath of cool fresh air, reminding myself that I was lucky to be alive.

I had passed out, and nearly drowned in a few inches of water. The realisation of the stupidity of my actions which had caused this incident to happen, made me feel like I was ungrateful and undervaluing of my life and everything and everyone in it.

I had always been so sensible and in control, so since when did I become so irresponsible?

Rewinding a year, I was fortunate enough to be invited on a university trip to Delhi in India. With a keen interest in business operations and processes, this trip gave me the opportunity to see first-hand how India's financial institutions operated and also explore the incredible and insightful culture that the country offered.

But, not only did the trip impact on me from an educational and cultural perspective, it also had a detrimental impact on my health and wellbeing and turned my world completely upside down.

Before the trip, I had started visiting the gym a few times a week and enjoyed a varied and healthy diet. I was always busy – with uni work, seminars, lectures, 3 jobs and a house to run – so keeping my weight down at that time came quite naturally and with little effort. I used my gym and swim visits as thinking time, to get away from the chaos of life.

After the trip, my life was a different story. As well as bringing home memories of an impactful experience, myself and many of my classmates also brought home 'Delhi Belly' (which is a severe stomach bug that sticks around for a long time!).

Due to this I couldn't keep any food or drink down for a good month after the trip, and following the end of the severe sickness and diarrhoea, and the excruciating painful stomach cramps (which kept me up most nights, taking away the sleep I desperately craved to regain energy to keep up with my busy lifestyle) I was unable to eat a diet of anything other than dried toast, cereal, tuna and crackers, which soon became boring and difficult to swallow, let alone stomach!

So, I started to want to eat less and less, and my previous love and enjoyment of food was now non-existent. At first, limiting my food intake and what I ate was a necessity to prevent the dreaded 'Delhi Belly' from flaring up, however it soon slipped into becoming an obsession, and even became a challenge, where I would see how many days I could go without giving in to the hunger pains.

Within 6 months I could manage about 3 days without eating any food and only consuming water, and for this I'd praise myself when seeing the weight drop off, going from a large size 12 [UK] to a small size 10 in this short time. Even though this was the case, I had the urge that I needed to do more. So instead of my usual 2 x 1-hour gym visits per week, this rapidly increased to 5-6 x 2-3 hour sessions, and 4-5 x 1 hour swim sessions per week – plus runs twice a day and lengthy rides on my exercise bike whenever I was at home.

To put it simply, many areas of my life were sacrificed for exercise. Time with my family and friends, meal times, housework and even some work days (where I could get away with it) would become replaced by some sort of physical exercise.

My brain was consumed with thoughts of food and exercise, and nothing else got a look in. My work suffered, my education suffered, my sleep suffered, and I was so exhausted that my concentration slipped and all I could focus on was the negative feelings I had about my body.

When I started on my journey with anorexia and exercise addiction I enjoyed losing weight, and I loved the way I felt in my new slimmer body. But, over time, every time I saw myself in a mirror all I could see was how large I looked, and I absolutely hated myself. And as I got skinnier the self-hate just grew and grew, to the point that I couldn't even face looking at myself anymore. I had to undress in the dark and wear the baggiest clothes I owned so I didn't have to look down and see my atrocious body.

Another 6 months had passed, and I was now in small size 8 clothes, and weighed just over 7 stone (which was a total loss of around 5 and a half stone since my India visit).

Fast-forwarding again to stepping out of that shower cubicle, I emerged a new woman. Still shaking from shock and shivering from the cold bathroom air, I stood staring at myself in the mirror and just sobbed, for hours. My world stopped at that moment. Time stood still. My unrealistic view on my body lifted and I just saw a scrawny, pale, skeleton staring back at me. I noticed my face was drawn, and my eyes were sunken, red, and bloodshot, with dark circles, as tears rolled and rolled continuously down my cheeks.

People say that when you come close to death you experience feelings of gratitude and thanks for your life, and I certainly did. These feelings were enough to pull me out of the pit of my illness and, once I admitted it to my family, they supported me to gradually eat healthily and exercise safely to become stronger with a more stable state of mind.

When I look back, the struggle to get better was harder than the challenge of starving, and the intenseness of excessive exercise. Therefore, when people criticise someone for having an eating disorder and just say 'eat more' this is certainly easier said than done. Eating disorders are both mental and physical illnesses that take work, support and time to heal.

And now I end the story, in 2018. Ten years on I am a size 14-16, after having 2 incredible children. I eat well and healthily, and enjoy playing with the children and walking my dog, in between rushing about in my (still) busy lifestyle.

Even though I am larger than I have been before, I am proud of my body – all the rolls, scars, stretch marks, cellulite, spots and redness make up me and stand for the huge challenges I have faced in my 30 years of life: pregnancy, childbirth, family celebrations, romantic meals, exciting holidays and fun days out have all shaped who I am today, and my eating disorder and exercise addiction also adds to that, so I am not ashamed of it at all...I am proud of overcoming it and becoming a stronger person because of it.

Serena Fordham – Author, Speaker, Entrepreneur and Business Owner of Glow Virtual Assistants, For HER, Her Business Brew and Norfolk Mums.

www.for-her.co.uk

Ari Snaevarsson, from Virginia, US, is Kinda Proud of his journey from body-building to body-loving

A common misunderstanding is that disordered eating only affects women, but the pressures to 'look' or 'perform' a certain way are just as likely to affect men. We are so grateful to Ari for sharing his difficult journey with us in order to raise awareness around this issue, and to give hope to other boys or men who might be in a similar situation and in need of support...

From bodybuilding to body-loving: My struggle through, and recovery from, Binge-Eating Disorder

When I was 17 I competed in my first bodybuilding show. I worked my way down to a pretty low energy intake pretty early on in the process, and for the last 5-6 weeks of prep (which was an 18-week ordeal). My life had become completely consumed by restriction and over-exercising. I was eating only "clean" foods at certain hours, a schedule I wouldn't let anything else get in the way of (including friends and family). I was doing way too much cardio, I was using absurd amounts of stimulants to muster up just enough energy to not pass out in class, I obsessed over my weigh-ins and let numbers on a scale turn into emotional events, and I had successfully isolated myself completely.

My sex drive, energy, and mood for the last 5 weeks were all in the tank. I was not a pleasant person to be around. But the worst part was the hunger. It was like nothing I'd ever experienced, and yet the thought of "letting" myself eat was almost equally disgusting to me. In class, I would scroll through pictures of "food porn" and write lists of foods I'd binge on, and in what order, after the show. I used to watch classmates eating and become sincerely angry. I would sometimes, after a long and emotional day, sneak into the pantry and "pig out" on literally one squeeze of honey, which would freak me out and cause me to compensate with an impromptu cardio session.

47

THE SHOW AND THE AFTERMATH

Immediately after stepping off stage at my show, I began eating. It started with some "fit pizzas" one of the booths at the venue was offering. We then hit a Hardee's, where I got one of the "monster" double-quarter-pounder burgers, cheesy fries, and a large soda. On the way back to the hotel, I distinctly remember virtually inhaling these cheesy fries and beginning to feel the most unnerving of sensations: my stomach was pleading for me to stop while my brain was yelling at me to keep eating. The mismatch between my biological satiety cues and brain-derived reward and taste demands was a scary feeling to have, as I was constantly unsure of which excruciating sensation to respond to.

Back at the hotel, I began binge-eating all the foods I had stocked up on for this purpose. This included Oreos, Reese's pieces, a half-gallon of chocolate milk, marshmallow peeps, peanut butter, protein bars, Fibre One brownies, moon pies, Gatorade, and more. As I continued to shovel this food into my mouth, my fullness turned into unbearable physical pain. I was incredibly nauseous and tried to sleep it off. But about two hours of sleep later, I was up and immediately began craving these foods again, so what did I do? Eat. And eat. And keep eating.

The night carried on like this: eating until I was in too much pain to keep going, trying to sleep, waking up to keep eating, etc. By the time the morning rolled around, I was binge-eating all of the free breakfast I could get. We then stopped at a pizza place before heading back home, where I proceeded to eat an entire pan pizza. This pattern persisted for a week straight. I was more depressed than I'd ever been at any point in my life prior.

HOW LOOKING AT MYSELF IN A HOTEL MIRROR CHANGED MY ENTIRE LIFE

Exactly one week after the show, I was getting out of the shower and saw myself in the full-length mirror in the bathroom. Though I had been taking "progress photos" of myself habitually since starting prep, and therefore had technically seen myself shirtless quite a few times after starting this binge, this was the first time I really saw myself and how "bad" I'd let things get. I had devoted 18 weeks of my life to extreme obsession centred around getting as lean as humanly possible, which involved cutting off friends and alienating family, letting myself fall into deep pits of depression, abusing stimulants, hours and hours and hours of cardio, and constant restriction. And so, seeing myself literally right back to where I was when I started was difficult to swallow.

I distinctly remember this moment, almost six years ago now, as I started sobbing profusely and could think of nothing to do other than go to bed and hope the pain would go away. I felt trapped and alone and like I'd never be able to express these worries to anyone.

MY RECOVERY

My recovery was not a formal, nor linear, process. In fact, I competed one more time, 3 years later, and went through a similar ordeal. But, over time, I was able to get to the point where I'm at now: no longer valuing myself based on how much I weigh, how much food I ate today, or even how well my workout went.

Since I hadn't even understood that what I went through was an eating disorder, the approaches I used that got me to this point were hardly the typical "ED recovery" techniques. Nonetheless, I learned that some general principles and practices were essential for my growth towards true intuitive eating and unconditional love of my body. These included a period of fundamental self-discovery, mindfulness meditation, learning to mindfully eat, improving my ability to see the bigger picture, focusing more on self-compassion than 'self-improvement', and some other various elements (all of which guided the instructions I give in my book on ED recovery, 100 Days of Food Freedom).

And so that is why I'm here, writing this story. Whilst the diet industry grows more and more, and cons people who just want to love the bodies they're in out of their money and out of their sense of security, there is a void in the nutrition field that needs to be filled. Food freedom means not defining ourselves by how "good" we did today in terms of diet or exercise, and it means not letting the scale control our lives. More accurately, food freedom involves loving the eating experience, separating our thoughts and emotions from our actions and beliefs, and ultimately treating our body with the respect it deserves.

Ari is a nutrition coach who works primarily with clients who suffer from disordered eating patterns. He also works as a counsellor, dietetic technician, and on-call facilities manager at a residential eating disorder treatment centre. In both capacities, he helps clients develop positive relationships with food and their bodies. Ari's book: "100 Days of Food Freedom: A Day-by-Day Journey to Self-Discovery, Freedom from Dieting, and Recovery from Your Eating Disorder", outlines a simple, day-by-day process to recovery from one's eating disorder.

Follow Ari's work at:

www.100doff.com

Instagram: @100daysoffoodfreedom,
Facebook: www.facebook.com/100doff/

Katie is Kinda Proud of her Fight Club badges to BEAT disordered eating

As Katie from Wiltshire, UK, so rightly states: 'recovery' from any form of psychological distress is never perfect, linear or uncomplicated. However, we can still have things to be proud of amidst the journey; any achievements help to build confidence and bring us a step closer to transforming our lives.

Here, Katie shares how creating her Fight Club pin badges, in collaboration with the eating disorder charity Beat, has given her something to not only be proud

of, but has connected her to others who are openly com-
mitted to overcoming their own struggles, to show they
are not alone…

Recovery is a strange concept when applied to an eating disorder. By definition, recovery means 'a return to a normal state of health, mind or strength' but, as I and many like me know, there is likely never going to be a complete abolition of our eating disorder. They are so unhelpfully entwined with our identities, our self-esteem, our subconscious, that to assume they disappear completely is, sadly, just unrealistic.

I say this with a painfully fresh perspective. 7 months ago I was fully 'recovered', yet now I am stuck in a full-blown relapse. It caught me completely off-guard and I still can't quite get my head around the fact it's happening. It is the first time I have ever relapsed completely, and I was truly in a place where I believed that anorexia would never affect me again. It was just a painful, sad, distant memory. I am a Mother to 2 young children, and of course Mums don't get anorexia, it completely undermines a Mother's inbuilt instinct to put her children first. So when I finally decided to undertake a 'healthy eating plan' early in 2018, I never believed that it would escalate into anything more. How wrong I was. Anorexia quickly sunk its claws in, tightened its grip, and took me over.

I am all too conscious that this seems a very negative start to something intended to incite hope, but the point I want to make is that when it comes to recovery, it pays to be realistic. It is seldom perfect, linear and uncomplicated. Allow yourself bad days, weeks even, as long as your resolve is there. Don't put pressure on yourself to recover perfectly...you know, the way people on Instagram recover, emerging from the dark as a beautiful butterfly and conveniently with the budget for 5 star hotel breaks and Michelin star meals. Recovery is whatever it looks like to you. This could be a night out with the girls without a single care about the sugar in the cocktails, a meal out with your family without the anxiety and forward planning, an ice cream on the beach with your children without worrying about them trying to kiss you with their ice- cream-covered mouths.

Remaining hopeful during recovery can be one of the biggest challenges. It is such a gruelling and often lengthy process that remaining optimistic and even remembering the end goal can feel impossible. This is why, straight off the back of watching a harrowing documentary on anorexia, I decided to try and do something to help support anyone suffering. I came up with the idea of designing pin badges – a small, subtle, portable reminder that you're committed to recovery, and not alone.

I approached the wonderful charity Beat to see if they'd be interested in getting involved and attaching their name to my project. To my wonderment, they responded , and with such enthusiasm that I decided to take the plunge. This was uncharacteristically bold of me, as my self-doubt usually results in me ducking out of anything that's remotely risky or reliant on my success. With the target of getting them ready for EDAW (Eating Disorders Awareness Week) in place, I went about designing them.

My work as an artist is largely influenced by nature, and I knew I wanted the pin badges to stay in keeping with this. I also really enjoy using symbolism, which suited the fact I wanted them to be subtle. I started thinking about the key messages I wanted to convey, not forgetting those supporting us, because they have it hard too. I started with dogwood, which symbolises love undiminished by adversity. This is a nod to the carers, families and friends who have to deal with someone they love trying to self-destruct, often whilst transforming into a completely different person, for being there regardless. Not through force or out of duty, but because they love you so much and are committed to your happiness.

Next, I wanted to use a mushroom to symbolise resilience. This one is fairly self-explanatory. It's no secret that recovering from an eating disorder is exceptionally difficult. If you are attempting to take on an eating disorder, you are already stronger than you think.

Finally, there's the moth, which symbolises intuition. Our intuition is a powerful and mystical tool that enables us to judge when something just isn't right. Trust yourself and your intuition in your recovery, harness your own voice to help empower yourself and belittle the eating disorder. If you're in contact with somebody who's struggling, and you think something doesn't seem right, it probably isn't. Don't be afraid to confront this, they'll thank you eventually for finding them out.

Thanks to Beat sharing my badges, and through my own promotion, over 330 fighters have purchased a badge. I couldn't be more thrilled with the response and every time I send one out, I feel proud of that person for acknowledging the struggle and taking it on. I have one on every one of my coats, and whenever I catch a glimpse of it in a mirror or window I can smile for a second and remember that I'm part of an amazing club of people fighting to make life better.

I will continue to fight and share my journey. I am starting treatment imminently and, with the support of my partner, I am pushing through what I hope has been the lowest point of this relapse. I hope to look back on this relapse as a reminder that I need to put myself first sometimes, keep my wits about me, and never underestimate an eating disorder or, more importantly, myself.

If you would like to find me on social media, or purchase a Fight Club pin badge, the links below will get you there!

Love to you all, we can do this together

Follow Katie: @edfightclub on Instagram and Twitter

Denise is KindaProud that she was brave enough to look at the roots of her compulsive eating, and love herself enough to heal

As Denise so eloquently writes, what often begin as our coping mechanisms in response to some kind of trauma, can develop into unhealthy compulsions which we need to look beneath to discover the roots of the pain. Turning the pain into our 'friend rather than foe' can be the turning point on the road to transformation. It's often a long and challenging process, but as Denise says, she has done it, and so can you ...

57

Well Springs Within

I am currently re-reading 'The Gift of Our Compulsions' by Mary O'Malley. In a nutshell the book encourages us to see our compulsions as Gifts; gifts because if we can stay still enough to understand them, we would find that at the heart of compulsion is a deep Wellspring waiting to fulfil and nourish our every need as no external thing ever truly can. No compulsion can give us the relief that we deep down need; or even the relief we initially experienced when we first engaged in the compulsive behaviour. It is this very inability that makes the behaviour compulsive as it can never reach the underlying legitimate need.

Finding relief in compulsions is a bit like expecting eating a banana will quench your thirst when it is a drink that the body needs. Indeed, the only thing the banana can do is temporarily distract us from how thirsty we are. You can't fool the body, though we can spend our whole lifetime trying. The body knows what it needs and will come back to get it. The body is well equipped at doing its job and is as equally committed to it. And its job? Keeping us well and strong, across the board. We give the body very little credit for this. Both we and the world very easily turn the body into 'enemy' then go on to treat it pretty badly, like it's a robot without feeling and need.

In Mary O'Malley's book we are also encouraged to not only change the way we view compulsions, but also to change the way we relate to them; bringing the light of much needed understanding and compassion to them, as they initially came into being to help us deal with and manage some great big difficult something. So, there's a way in which compulsions can be more readily resolved simply by seeing compulsions as more friend than foe, and in so doing, paradoxically take the sting out of them.

Compulsions come to go, being set up to serve us at one time, not for all our lifetime. The process of allowing them to pass is not an easy one considering the condition of compulsion's ferocious appetite: not easy, although possible.

It is a testimony to how far I have come in my general healing journey, as well as in my recovery from disordered eating, that I have not fallen back into bulimia's misguided and crippling embrace, because currently, and ongoing for a good few years, I have a couple of life events that are truly testing me. In the past these situations/triggers would have been good enough reason for me to fall back into my struggles with food; but I simply refuse to. Recovery wise, I have come too far to fall at this hurdle, and I am still 100% committed to living my best life possible, especially after a childhood marred by abuse. The good news is, which I ought to remember and feel more proud of myself about, in the old eating disorder days (12 – 22 years old) I would have binged and purged for much less!

The only thing about my eating that can concern

me a little at times is, on occasion, I can still tend toward emotional eating. But overall, like I said, I have a very good handle on my eating, and that is the way I want to keep it, not least of all because I've put a great deal of energy and effort into my recovery and healing from Bulimia.

Being well on the recovery road, I can tolerate and contain my, at times, internal angst and delay, and not engage those inner compulsive drives, in a way I never could at the beginning of giving up bulimia and happening on the recovery road. I know that these difficult and painful feeling states can and do pass and I am now more familiar with the felt experience of their transmutation. So, I no longer stand in the way of the process because the reward and relief gained from this level of self-acceptance feeds and sustains me better than compulsively acting out ever did, or ever could.

I am currently re-reading Mary O'Malley's book because, like I said, I am feeling challenged on a number of fronts and I want to ensure that compulsions don't try to sneak in through internal, unconscious, back doors. I want to keep that bolt on, as my suffering does not need, or deserve, more suffering added on!

In regard to self-care, I do all those mind, body and spiritual things to keep me well, like exercise, meditation, healthier eating, living more in the moment, and having greater self-appreciation and presence in my day-to-day life. I have also taken to, these past 6 weeks, gifting myself with a 'PJ stay in bed all day Saturday'. Even this is an achievement in and of itself as another one of my compulsions has been 'overdoing' and 'keeping busy'. Initially I had found taking this particular 'fear of being still' monkey off my back was difficult; taking it off my back and simply being, relaxing and doing no-thing in particular...

Being still and allowing myself relaxation at first felt incredibly painstakingly angst-filled, as well as mind-numbingly boring. Now that painful 'Insperience' has too been mostly transformed from restless haunting into something that fills me more with Peace and Joy. *Just being* in the moment and enjoying it for all it's worth, has been worth all the difficult feelings that initially accompanied doing no-thing. Sometimes it still takes me a minute or two to 'come down' after being way too busy and up in my head for too long, but I now know the rewards of Mr & Mrs Peace and Joy.

All is a process and takes time. It's taken me 33 years to be where I am today. It has also taken time to more fully realise that The Soul Food and The Joy is *in* the journey, not the destination. So, try not to worry yourself too much because, as such, we already have all the time in the world that we need, and we don't have to wait 'until' some future date to truly *In Joy* our lives and Be Our True Selves. To quote the author:

"I am not offering you a cure; that is the old style of thinking in which your healing happens sometime in the future. This process is about inviting you into relationship with what is right now, (difficult or otherwise), for that is where true healing lies."

Like a child reaching to be picked up by her mummy and be given her mother's time - which probably was the kind of thing that was missing and/or lacking when compulsion first came knocking - we need to learn to reach down, pick ourselves up, and respond to our needs in more loving, appropriate and self-soothing ways. Why? Because we are worth it! And if you don't know, I know it for you!!

Peace & Love, Light,

Denise

Denise is a mother of 2 sons and overjoyed grandmother of 4. She currently works as a Counsellor counselling women who have experienced Domestic and Sexual violence, and has a small Private Practice. She has a huge belief in the transformative power of creativity and learning and growing through the sharing of experiences, of which her life bares testimony.

Read Denise's blog and find out about her upcoming autobiography, here:

https://fromtheheartsoul.wordpress.com

Email: andstillirise9@outlook.com

Brave Becky is Kinda Proud of emerging through a history of bullying and self-harm

As Becky bravely demonstrates through recounting her own story, recovery isn't a linear process with a definite 'end'. It's most likely an ongoing development of self-awareness, including needing to embrace self-love and self-acceptance over the opinions of others. Healthy body weight and shape/size is different for every individual, so learning to be happy in our own skin is the most important factor. As Becky says, finding your 'tribe' - people with whom you can be yourself and who accept you as you are - can be a life-changing step to healing...

So here goes, my story of recovery. I won't go into everything and you know what, that's OK. No matter who you tell your story to, you should only tell as much as you feel comfortable.

I grew up feeling very different to others. I was bullied every day and couldn't seem to do anything to fit in, so I started just doing what I enjoyed. Sadly, the bullying didn't stop and continued throughout my childhood. This of course impacted my self-esteem and confidence and I tended to hide away. I focused on my art and music that I connected with. I was even isolated at home and would stay in my room. I struggled with the emotions I felt and could not find a way to express them, so I turned to self-harm as a way to cope. When this was discovered this was also met with hostility and mocking. I withdrew further and struggled to connect with others.

As I grew older I focused a lot on what I ate, as I could control this aspect of my life more than most others. When I went to college all the years of being called fat, ugly and worthless caught up with me. That's all I could see. Looking back, I was about a size 8, which for my tall height isn't ideal, but I would grab skin and be convinced it was fat. I ate barely anything. It wasn't until I kept losing weight and people started to notice and comment on how unwell I looked that I started to realise. I started to eat a bit more but still struggled with body image and my confidence was still so low. My friend suggested I try modelling, which helped a bit as I was getting positive feedback on my style. I enjoyed the outfits and getting made up.

However, it could also be a point of conflict for me, as I would compare myself to others and how they looked. I still didn't feel in control, so I became very fixated on getting top grades and this became my way of 'being worthwhile'. This continued throughout uni and I felt I'd 'fail' if I didn't get a First. I started counselling and later had CAT (Cognitive Analytical Therapy) and I slowly started to improve. I still really struggled with confidence, but it was improving.

As I grew older and found people with similar interests and those who didn't judge me, I improved more. I wouldn't say I'm the most confident or body-confident individual, but I've come a long way and no longer hate myself. I accept myself for who I am and do my best to put love into the world. I support vulnerable adults as I don't want anyone to feel like I did growing up.

We are all always growing, but if we can recognise our negative past thought patterns and can learn from them, we can move forward. With support I've now not self-harmed in nearly 8 years, something I never thought possible. I'm not super-happy with my weight, but I'm not ugly, I feel like I'm a healthy size for me...I wouldn't say I love my body, but I appreciate it. I've used tattoos to make my scars into what I see as transformation, and I find this beautiful. I'm grateful for all I learned and those who have supported me on my journey. Where there are shadows, there is also light. We can use this knowledge to help others and help heal ourselves.

Becky now works supporting the disadvantaged in her local community, using her personal experiences as a foundation for her non-judgemental approach to all aspects of life.

Ivy found the answers for her healing lay in the darkness, not in her appearance

You may recognise Ivy, now happily based in Florida, from the #EmergingProud film. Hospitalised due to a spiritual awakening unearthing unconscious trauma for healing, Ivy was once mute – the only way she was able to express herself was through her art. Now, Ivy has created a business with the coping mechanism that she loves; as she says, in her darkness she found herself and the path to her future…

Early childhood to me felt so wonderful. I was taught unconditional love by being given unconditional love. My heart was so full and my spirit so carefree. I had two loving parents, a brother, sisters, cousins, lots of family and friends. School was good for me; even though I was a bit shy I was an excellent student and a pretty good athlete.

I was truly blessed.

Then at some point I became depressed. Family turmoil and separation occurred when life, work and everything lost balance. Loss of balance and lack of the ability to feel love made me lose the key to my heart. But this was not so true, I later found out.

Art, learning, and continued love and support from others helped me through my dark spaces. Tragedy took blow after blow, I seemed to rise and fall with each obstacle like the hurdles in track and field, but true love grounded me every time I got lost.

At some point I developed an eating disorder in all of this. I received some mixed messages from my environment about what I ought to look like and how that should make me feel about myself... Some of it came from magazines, some of it from kids at school, some from TV or even innocent bystanders who meant me no harm.

So I began to binge and purge, and restrict... My two-sided reward was soon attained, so I thought, when I saw myself become thinner. As I looked more 'beautiful', I felt more love. I needed that so much that I became addicted to self-judgement and self-deprecation. I loved everyone else around me so much but I couldn't seem to love myself enough to take good gentle care of myself. Then one day I fell in love. I fell in love and found true love outside of myself, outside of my comfort zones with the man of my dreams. I never expected this to ever happen. So much heartache made me doubt if true love existed. But here it was. And I was so happy to care for someone, that together we began to take such good care of each other. In giving and loving, I received love and my heart was full once again. This natural heart fulfillment healed my soul, but there was still work to to do. So much work. I still deep down believed that my beauty was only skin deep, that it could easily fade and with that my value as a person would be downgraded. That was the lie that I once believed and had to work my way through.

It wasn't easy, but with proper love and support, compassion and understanding, and a little courage, I learned to love myself and forgive myself as well as others, no matter what. Perfectionism has new meaning. I no longer wish to be perfect, I wish to feel perfect as I am, with room to grow. With true love, I found myself again in all my dark spaces, and opened the door to new friendships. I found that it was not that hard to love myself after all and, if I stumbled, I had so many wonderful people to help lift me back up.

Returning the favor and giving back has become my

pleasure and purpose. True love, self love, and an open heart, though heavy at times, is so worth it. I am a work in progress, and I love my beautiful mess!

Ivy now channels her passion for helping others into creating art and has recently started an organic creative business, ORDERGANIC (www.orderganic.com). With her husband Eddie they grow a variety of organic culinary and medicinal herbs, vegetables, fruits, and create all-natural organic body products.

Food was once her dark obsession, but now Kam works with healthy nutrition to empower others

Kam Sokhi from West Sussex, UK has transformed her life by healing emotional wounds from the past that she was trying to control through food; it was only through facing those wounds that Kam was able to emerge through her darkness, which has led to her empowering others to do the same. Here, Kam bravely tells her story to give hope…

I was just an ordinary 13-year old when my older sister and I made a pact to lose weight.

I became very competitive. My sister, 'the golden child', got all the good grades and I felt I'd never match her. My dad would tell me I was stupid, I'd amount to nothing and that I was a failure! The only thing, in my mind, that I could do better than her was to lose weight.

Living in a strict Indian household, we were never really allowed out; it certainly was not ok to wear makeup or have boyfriends. If I dared answer back, I'd get a good beating. My dad had no problem exercising his control over us either verbally or physically. Life was all about religion, our family and our education.

Now I could control how much I ate and I found I was really good at it. I'd feel so proud I'd only consumed an apple and a litre of diet coke for days. I became sneaky at hiding food and obsessed with exercise. I was getting noticed at school because I was so thin; I was ecstatic.

It didn't matter that I hadn't had a period for two years, or that some days I'd swallow a hundred slimming pills AND tens of laxatives. I'd binge and purge. An average binge would last for hours and I could eat 10 chocolate bars, 5 ice creams, 7 packets of crisps, not to mention the rest. I weighed 5 stone at age 15 and was wearing children's clothes. My bones were protruding and my hair fell out, yet when I looked in the mirror all I could see was a fat, ugly person staring back at me.

At my lowest point, I considered killing myself. There were times when I self–harmed and the relationship with my father became worse. I began rebelling: smoking, drinking, dabbling in drugs, sometimes running away from home.

Then, I was busted at school. My best friend dobbed me in to my parents; told them I was throwing my lunch away. Things began to change, the visits to the doctor started, as did a year of psychiatric hospital care with an eating disorder specialist. These interventions inevitably brought my bulimia and anorexia to an end.

But in the years to come, my obsession with food and exercise continued. I felt I was never perfect and continued with strict eating regimes. I'd categorise foods as good or bad and if I ever ate anything from the bad list then I would ricochet into self-loathing. My laxative abuse was still prevalent, as was the occasional habit of taking slimming pills or going on detox diets. I was in my thirties now and still very self-conscious about my body image, not ever going swimming or dancing in public.

The pivotal moment in my recovery was meeting an iridologist who told me I had to give up sugar. She'd explained, I'd been replacing the sweetness of life with sugar, though if I started to love myself the weight would drop off! I had no idea what she was talking about and it would be ten years until I fully understood what she meant.

As I was a chef I thought I'm creative, I'll just create some new recipes and I'll be fine. In fact, a whole new world opened up. I started a clean, healthy way of eating and even started a Facebook page, sharing recipes. I started experimenting, making raw desserts. For the first time ever, guilt-free eating with no self-loathing afterwards; it really was a revelation!

I also suffered from food allergies. This was yet another challenge. Being vegan as well, you can imagine how regimented and strict my life was around food.

Through the IPE eating psychology coaching course I've found the healing I've so needed. I discovered that being fast, rigid, strict and militant in my eating habits, is a reflection of how I conducted my life in general. I learned that weight gain is a form of self-protection and that self-confidence isn't going to magically appear once I'm thin; after all, being skinny made me just as miserable. Being happy in myself and with my body image, by healing the emotional wounds from the past, is the key.

Now, it's time to give back, to help other women find freedom from the guilt and shame felt around food. My commitment is to empower women to become the best version of themselves; to find confidence and peace within, no matter their size, and transform their view of life, themselves and their relationship with food. I guide and support their weight loss journey and help them sustain that weight loss while being healthy, respectful and loving to themselves both physically and emotionally.

What a great gift is that!

Warmly,

Kam, Eating Psychology Coach

CHEF-NLP-NUTRITION

Empowering women to become

The best version of themselves

Find out more about Kam and her work here...

https://m.facebook.com/Kam-eating-Psychology-coach-656341857763098/

https://www.instagram.com/kam_eatingpsychology_coach/

Shae from Hawaii now nourishes herself with Self-love

Through her studies, Shae has come to realise how interrelated our self-care is to the environment and the planet. She says: 'It was this love that I had for myself, even in the very beginning of my journey, that allowed and influenced my transformation'.

Here Shae shares her transformation journey from a negative self-image to allowing herself to devote valuable time to her needs, desires, pleasures, and inspiration...

76

"And I said to my body, softly, 'I want to be your friend.' It took a long breath and replied, 'I have been waiting my whole life for this."

—Nayyirah Waheed

When I was 8, my first memory of feeling negatively self-conscious of my body, was when my mom saw me touching the skin on my belly and she asked me if I was playing with my rolls. I am not sure why she referred to my belly as "rolls" because I was a slim, healthy young girl. However, I do not recall having a specific body image prior to that comment and it planted a seed that followed me throughout childhood and well into adulthood. I began to gain weight and binge-eat occasionally during my teens. My weight fluctuated and I gained and lost around 30 pounds through my early 20s. When I moved into a cottage alone and was working at a law firm I hated, I gained a lot of weight in a couple of years. I was on my own and completely uninspired.

I ended up deciding to break free from city life and move up to a quaint, small town in the mountains to attend a community college that had a horse program (I trained and bred horses throughout my teens and 20s). During college, I met the man who would become my husband and the love of my life. We married and had our daughter. After our daughter was born in 2003, my husband and I experienced extraordinary difficulties and challenges from external circumstances that forced us to live apart for years. The stress of missing my love and raising our daughter alone caused me to become obese. I spent most of those years in survival mode. There was a period of time I was alone and homeless with my one-year-old. We camped for a whole summer until school resumed and we moved into a homeless shelter before finally being able to find an affordable home.

Life for my toddler and I smoothed out as the rhythmic school routine set in. It was during this phase that I tried extreme measures to lose weight and regain health and self-love. I tried teas and diets and read everything I could get a hold of to try and solve my "problem." I would do well for a while and then slip back into self-sabotaging habits. I graduated and transferred to a four-year university. We stayed there for a year and I transferred again to Mills College in Oakland. My daughter and I lived there for two years on campus in Family Housing until I graduated and moved again. At this point we were living with my husband again and moving a lot.

I continued on in school and was accepted into a doctoral program. The financial, emotional, and academic stress was overwhelming. I never stopped trying to get control of my weight and I also never stopped loving myself. I was disappointed with myself but practiced self-love and was generally gentle with my process. I remember feeling more desperate and depressed than angry and hating myself.

The doctoral program began to require my cohort to focus on our research interests and mine was mindfulness. I loved that it encompassed so many
78

aspects of life and had such a positive impact on people who use mindfulness techniques. Eventually, I narrowed my focus to mindful eating and my dissertation design unfolded to include human and planetary health and our food system politics, which was all framed within mindful eating. The experience of researching and writing my dissertation was extremely rewarding and an amazing journey. I felt, and still feel, that I found my life's mission. Also, during that time, I became a certified health coach. It was at this point in my journey I finally found my balance.

Nourishing one's body is a significant aspect of what it is to be human. I believe that finding ways to connect more intimately with the body, food, the eating process, and the ways in which they are all connected to the environment, is purposeful and worthwhile. If these connections are made, I believe the heightened awareness may cultivate improved physical and environmental health. In my research I learned so much about how a plant-based diet improves health and it just resonated with me. I deeply believe in the power of the connection between how food is grown and produced and the ways it is interrelated with the environment and planetary health.

Once I began eating whole food plant-based diet, my body began to feel so vibrant and alive. My digestion was on point and my sleep patterns fell into a satiating rhythm. All health issues disappeared within a few months. I began walking regularly and enjoying yoga in the mornings. Another piece of my healing was committing to a regular meditation practice first thing in the morning. I made it my first self-care priority. This practice was paramount in my transformation. It has been one of the most powerful aspects of coming back into balance. Another very important facet of my transformation has been spending time with loved ones. When I was overweight and feeling depressed all those years, I did not have a desire to spend a lot of time with my family and friends. This fell away almost immediately when I changed my self-sabotaging habits.

Realizing that it was my habits that held me out of balance with my body-mind, I did a lot of research on the subject of habits. I learned that most of us are three days away from making positive and sustainable habitual changes. In other words, it is especially hard for three days and then as our internal audience becomes more impressed with our new and healthier habits, the transition becomes easier and the momentum begins. I take each day at a time. This is what mindfulness teaches. My goal each morning is to do things that specific day that will make me feel healthy, strong, joyful, and clear-minded. Every morning, after meditation, I read a page of notes I created to remind me of all the inspirational reasons I have to continue my healthy habits this day. I only focus on the present day and try not to ruminate on the past or future unless it is reminiscing on pleasant memories or daydreaming of pleasant future thoughts.

Over a couple of years, I have lost more than half

my body weight and completely transformed not only my body but the way I show up in the world and my life experience. I am free in my body now and I intentionally practice self-love and self-care everyday. This transformation really is an internal process. I find myself listening carefully to the subtle whisperings of my internal audience and the longer I do, the more love and health emanates from my Being. Self-love, for me, is listening to my authentic self and following through each day with the commitment I made to devote time to my needs, desires, pleasures, and inspiration. It was this love that I had for myself, even in the very beginning of my journey, that allowed and influenced my transformation.

Two mantras I say to myself daily:

~I am happy, healthy, calm, and beautiful.

~How rare and perfect you are.

Sally is embracing herself today, and encourages you to do the same

A childhood of bullying left Sally feeling like she didn't fit in. Now she has realised her happiness is found in embracing her authentic uniqueness, not in trying to squeeze herself into someone everyone else says she should be. We are Kinda Proud of you Sally!

Hi I'm Sally. I've always battled with low self-esteem and low feelings towards my body image, my weight, my size, my shape, my curves and my personality. It has worried me so much that I have felt at times that

I don't fit in; that I'm not 'normal'.

I was bullied so bad at school which affected my confidence too, way into adulthood. I was bullied because I was then a size 14, which is slimmer than I am now! The kids made my life hell because I was bigger than most others. I made out I was ill a few weeks to my mum so I didn't have to go to school. The kids used to say I was a sumo wrestler, I had thunder thighs etc...it was crippling but I didn't have the confidence to fight back. Then as I got older the bullying changed because I had curly hair !! Or because of the job my parents did, or the house we lived in...It was ridiculous and I grew up feeling like I didn't belong, or fit in, or that I wasn't accepted, as I didn't have many friends at school, or because I wasn't cool enough!

But it's only as I have grown older, that I've felt more comfortable with who I am, my journey, my body and where I am heading in life. The confidence came from getting older and understanding that I don't have to accept bullying from others about who I am - I am whole and complete - I am enough, I learnt I didn't have to fit in with anyone else or be like anyone else. My mum always encouraged me to be me and said things like 'everyone else is more concerned about what *they* look like, not what *you* look like!' This advice still sits with me now I'm an adult. It's still a learning curve to accept my body as it is, but I now accept it more and know that I am not just my physical body or my appearance, I am more than that. I have a soul, a being and energy inside too.

Once I left school that pressure of having to fit in, or be like everyone else faded and I began to find hobbies and interests in things that led me down various paths, and finally onto my spiritual path, where I have found most happiness in who I am and what interests me. My groups of friends changed and I found myself surrounded by people who enjoyed the same things as I did, and enjoyed me being myself...and I enjoyed and accepted them for who they were. This gave me great confidence and settled feelings.

I went to my first reiki session for my 30th birthday and loved it so much; a great turning point for me. I wanted to know and learn more and started looking into alternative therapies and ways of being. I discovered I enjoyed different things than others did at the time; I enjoyed learning new beliefs and practices. I started going to new groups and workshops and making a new circle of friends. So the feeling of having to fit in, or be slim or a certain way didn't matter anymore - what mattered was my happiness and wellbeing.

In 2013 I trained in reiki myself and it led me into learning other things that made me happy like sound therapy and mantras. Even with others' views and opinions on what I was training in, I understand now that it was others' perception and it didn't matter, only what made me happy mattered. Freedom came even more now to have the confidence to be me.

In the last few years I have started to embrace me more and not feel like I have to fit in with anyone. I have found groups of friends who have accepted me as I am, I have found hobbies, passions and purpose. This has all helped me realise I can be whoever I want to be, I don't have to be the same as everyone else, and I actually embrace now that I'm not!

I still have days where I don't love myself or my body, but I do love my journey and where I am in life and how I got here. I recently cut down my full-time job to part-time to concentrate more on doing what I love and working with people I want to; helping others, making time for what makes me happy and connected to myself. This includes doing regular yoga, or Qigong and not being hard on myself on the days I don't fancy it or don't have the time. I have also found chanting mantra helps me if I have a lot of stress or worries - it brings me peace, balance and harmony. I enjoy being around my like-minded friends and people I can connect with who share the same views on life.

The days of being bullied at school feel a long distant memory now. I wish I'd had the inner strength and confidence back then to follow my heart and be my true authentic self and not worry what others thought, but I've realised this is all part of my journey into making me who I am today and has all helped me to become the well-rounded unique person I am. Plus, I also have the most amazing curly hair which I now love and I colour it with fun colours which I feel matches who I am and my personality. This brings me freedom and happiness by being my authentic self. I still have wobble days about my body, like feelings of 'am I too curvy?Am I too fat ? Am I too out there and wacky?! But I think back and realise this is where I'm at right now, this is who I am right now; it may change and vary but this is me today. And that's all I can be - the real version of me on this day, however that day feels!

We are all on our own journeys,there is no need to compete for we are all unique and special in our own way, which isn't necessarily the same way as others are. I have found a love for things that bring me peace and balance, including yoga, meditation, chanting, music, sound therapy and alternative therapies that all help me to feel my true self. I see beauty in others that they may not see in themselves, and I'm sure people see beauty in me that I don't see in myself...

I am embracing me today and I dare you to do the same! xxx from Sally.

It took Stella needing to 'crack' with a health crisis to value her body as her temple

"The wound is where the light enters"
- **Rumi**

Sometimes it's the wisdom of our body that speaks to us the loudest. Like Stella, sometimes we are made to stop physically so we can learn the lessons we need to hear. Stella found happiness in the very thing she had been running from for so many years; now viewing her body as her temple in which she finds sanctuary and joy, she

has the courage not only to heal herself, but to also in-
spire others…

As far back as I can recall I felt out of place, different and uncomfortable in my skin. I had always had an unhealthy relationship with food and my body as a child. I would often over-eat, and I remember skiving off school because I was horrified that the only trousers I had to wear made me look fat. I was seven at the time. I hid those trousers like my feelings and no one found them.

When I was eleven an older girl showed me how to make myself sick. I can only imagine that it was a kind of bonding exercise but what she was actually sharing was a weapon: Bulimia was a young girl's weapon against the uncontrollable and confusing chaos of an adult world. By the time I was fifteen I was making myself sick regularly. Through binging I was letting myself lose control, it was always from a place of deep anxiety. Following this would come the purge, motivated by the shame of losing control and the need to regain it urgently. Not only for control's sake but also to adhere to an acceptable shape by society's standards. As a young woman, so much of my worth was placed on my body and that body was dictated to me by males and beauty images. The compulsion to eat I am sure was, and still is, about love, acceptance and comfort. It was born from confusion about what and who I was meant to be.

Over time my mental health improved and I would slip into bulimia less and less. In my early twenties I was well enough to have left it behind, and although I would still feel the compulsion, I would refuse to hurt my body. For me this was a radical concept, since I had never loved myself enough to lay that boundary of self-care. It was a start but there was a long way to go. At this stage I was still in denial that I had a problem. It was as if it was happening to someone else, I was detached from it. In not dealing with the issue of bulimia, let alone all the underlying causes, this familiar beast would soon grow a new head.

At twenty-five, during a time of upheaval and grief, I began dramatically changing my eating habits and focusing on vegetables, juicing and being healthy. I lost a lot of weight around this time and people commented on how thin I was with either concern or envy and it felt good. Over time this would develop into an unhealthy obsession with clean eating to the point where I would create strict rules on what I allowed myself to consume. I was skipping meals, restricting food groups and developing extreme beliefs around food. On a good day I was a healthy eater. On a bad day I was fixated by the idea that tumorous cells were multiplying inside me and the only way to prevent this was through cleansing my body with clean eating. Healthy eating is wonderfully healing but the extent to which I was obsessing was clearly not healthy. I would come to understand this obsession as orthorexia, a form of disordered eating that is becoming more recognised. I believe that the range of confusing and contradictory messages on health out there today are contributing to the growth

89

in people with this condition.

Just over a year ago, after months of chronic fatigue, I was diagnosed with M.E. and everything began to change. I had the opportunity to reassess my life, my priorities, and to make space for self-care. This health crisis cracked me open and sparked the realisation that I was, and had been for some time, in spiritual crisis. I started to explore mind-body connections and tried every holistic therapy I could find. I am delighted to say I am doing well and, although I will always have to manage my M.E. symptoms, I am happier than I have ever been. I know this to be down to re-learning how to connect with myself, my mind-body, my soul. Through these therapies and developing my own daily spiritual self-care practice I have begun to heal old wounds that previously consumed me and change my un-checked negative thought patterns.

A turning point was the realisation that if I kept telling my body it was ugly I would make it true. If I told my body that it was beautiful it would be beautiful - the power of thought really is transformative. I found my voice and unlearnt all that poor self-care that was really centred on fear and a lack of inner knowing. Only once I had rebuilt my foundation and learnt to really love myself, was I able to confront my relationship with food out in the open.

It will always be complicated and it will never go away. Some days are harder than others, but most days are pretty good. How I feel about myself today has little to do with the way I look and everything to do with self-love, acceptance and authenticity. In the past I was unkind to myself and taught others to follow my lead. Today I respect myself deeply and show others how I deserve to be treated, with the hope that I can inspire self-care in those who need it most.

My body is my soul's companion, it walks with me in this life and takes burdens and knocks along the way. It is not my prison, it is like a school in which I learn. It helps me reach new places. It is my temple in which I have sanctuary, comfort and joy. Give me courage to listen to my own story, to begin to know myself so that I can listen and be useful to others.

Kathleen Donhardt Emerges Proud to freely speak her beautifully real TRUTH

Kathleen from Mount Gambier, South Australia was inspired by our KindaProud Rep. Amy's story to share her own journey. We honour and respect Kathleen's bravery in beating guilt and shame to find her voice and inspire others through her own story...

For 48 years I have carried the SHAME and GUILT for childhood experiences. I have owned and retained the responsibility for what happened to me, wondering why I felt so guilty about so many experiences of abuse in my life - like being born into a home of domestic violence. It's easy to make the truth all about 'being provided for' and acknowledging 'they did their best with what they knew'.

The TRUTH is, it was traumatic being around the yelling, screaming and hitting that often ended with bruises, blood, breakages, tears and bitterness. Through a child's eyes it's terrifying not knowing if she's going to actually cut his throat with the knife she holds close.

It's easy to make the truth about a grade 1 teacher just doing her job. The TRUTH is, she was a bully who I was terrified of and I'd wet my pants over daring to ask her if I could go to the toilet. She was mean.

It's easy to make the truth all about being a liar because I stayed silent for so many years. The TRUTH is, he sexually abused me many times, and I was only about 7 or 8. I believed it was my fault and their accusations and denial of the truth cut deeper than the abuse.

It's easy to make the truth all about it being my fault, my shame that I was only 13 when I gave away my virginity because I didn't have the courage to walk away. The TRUTH is he conned me and raped me.

It's easy to make the truth about it being all my fault when I fell pregnant at barely 17. The TRUTH is it seemed to be my responsibility to tell not only my mother but his as well, and allow him to leave town first so he could get on with his precious life. I believed it was the least I could do as it was my fault, even though he was the one who had been pursuing me all those years.

It's easy to make the truth all about helping and supporting family because that's what you do. The TRUTH is they used and abused me for anything they could.

It's easy to make the truth that I've been overweight from a young age because I'm built 'just like my grandmother', or I'm lazy and eat too much like all fat people. The TRUTH is it's the trauma from all of the above and a tonne more that has set my body up to so beautifully 'protect' me from all the abuse, stress and trauma in the only way it knew how. Gain weight and hold on to it for dear life, to keep me safe. The TRUTH is those diets they made me do starting at age twelve, just kept helping me gain even more.

I AM grateful though - oh dearly I am so deeply grateful - for everything all of this taught me. I love and treasure the gifts, learning and growth it's provided me. Just like how I have fallen in love with me and my body on a whole new depth that is new and nourishing me emotionally, physically, spiritually. Never in my life have I felt safer around food than I do now. Never in my life have I felt safer in this world and in my own skin than I do now. Thirty two years of dieting helped me get so overweight, depressed and hating everything about myself, believing I was the problem. I have learned through these experiences, and a passionate search for the solutions, that it wasn't another diet I needed - it was actually a way to love and accept myself fully and deeply just as I am, for who I am, and the weight would fall away by itself, just as it is now.

Society shames anyone who dares to speak of sexual abuse, domestic violence, suicide, financial abuse, emotional abuse and this list goes on. It's the silencing and denial, which rapes us over and over of the freedom to be who we truly are; speaking freely of our life experiences regardless of what they are.

NOT ANYMORE - Not in my time, not in my life. I will continue to share my truth of how it was for me and the healing I've done to come through it. I will NEVER BE SILENCED because others are uncomfortable - that's what continues to feed the ongoing problem. It's the silence that allows it to keep happening over and over. I will speak on behalf of others, until they find their voice, their strength and their power. I am not a victim, I am not a survivor, I've lived through and from it. It's not my shame, it's not my guilt and I will no longer carry it.

I am far from perfect and nor do I strive to be; I have much to keep learning, growing and evolving with. That excites me a lot and today, right now, my heart is rich and my heart is full and I AM truly FREE to SPEAK MY TRUTH.

Kathleen Donhardt – Light Elephant Coach – Mount Gambier, South Australia

Follow Kathleen speaking her truth on these platforms:-

www.facebook.com/lightelephantcoach

www.instagram.com/lightelephantcoach

Https://passionfulfilledkmd.wordpress.com

Https://aulinkedin.com/in/kathleen-donhardt-163a7684

Meanha from Norwich stands up against Islamophobia as she 'Emerges' into her mission to be unapologetically herself

Emotional distress does not discriminate; discrimination causes emotional distress. Meanha courageously shares how being in a cultural minority has led to her being the victim of mindless attacks, and how these acts of ignorance led to her questioning herself causing mental health struggles.

Emotional pain connects us, it is the same whatever race,

culture, gender or sexuality we are. Pain unites us in our
shared humanity…and from that connection back to Self
and others we can rise into our mission, as Meanha is
now unapologetically doing…

Self-Esteem + Islamophobia = Mission

My experience is a conundrum of various different
issues that have contributed to my journey with
my mental health and self-respect. I don't think
anyone would be able to identify and blame any one
incident or event, rather it is a concoction of multiple
events and social-cultural factors that lead to the
disintegration of my mental health. Followed by a
venture of growth, discovery, resilience and being
unapologetically me.

Growing up in an all-white community, I stuck out
like a sore thumb. Being on the larger side and never
fitting in clothes made for girls my age didn't help
my self-confidence. As the years went by, I became
more and more obsessed with the way that I looked,
and how much I weighed and 'would people think
I'm too brown' if I ate that, wore this, or did/didn't
do that. Identity crisis was an understatement.

Around 13/14 I became desperate to just be like
everyone else, and it was a bitter taste every time I
failed to fit in. Something always made me different,
no matter how hard I tried to leave my religion,
culture, norms and values behind. I always tried to
make myself feel better about my friendship circles
despite being the friend with the 'exotic attitude'

eating the 'foreign food' with the 'Asian hair and skin', and of course the passive racism which I just swallowed with laughter. I had reached absolute rock bottom, and this was my earliest memory of experiencing feelings of worthlessness. I had the intense desire to just disappear.

After reconnecting with my faith around 15/16, I began to find peace in knowing that my purpose in life was not to serve society's ideals of how I should be, and Islam was the one thing that kept me anchored during these turbulent times. After I left school, I put on the hijab as I still feared being 'different'. When I donned the hijab, I felt so powerful and beautiful and I felt like no one could take away my shine and confidence. A few weeks later I received a few comments from 'friends' whom I later realised were not worth my time and energy, but their comments triggered something: 'Am I making myself *more* different?' I planted those thoughts to the back of my head, my hijab brought me more happiness in just a few weeks than it had in all my years of existence when I was living for other people and their preferences.

After becoming more and more closer to Islam, I wanted to gain better God Consciousness and whilst studying various things at college, I realised just how much our media and government capitalise off their consumers' lack of confidence and ability to be comfortable in their own skin. I did not want to be part of that. I decided to wear the Niqab (face veil), and I remember the first day I did. I felt so empowered and invincible. However, over time, my intentions changed. It became a way for me to be forgotten about and disappear in the back of the classroom. It became a way for me to be socially isolated as people refused to make eye contact with me or ask me for my opinions. It became a way for me to be silently judged in people's awkward glances which could be so loudly felt. I began to wonder again, 'had I done this to myself? Did I deserve this behaviour for being different again?'

In April 2014, I was verbally attacked by a man who claimed I was arrogant, and he was disgusted by what I stand for. He backed me into a shop corner and spat harsher words. I wasn't angry at him, he was ignorant, I was more upset and embarrassed at the fact that no one defended me. Not even the other Muslims who were standing and watching. I was disappointed and couldn't help wondering 'was I too different for them to stick up for me?'.

In May 2014, myself and a friend were physically attacked on the way home. It was broad daylight on a busy road. The woman who attacked us repeatedly said that we couldn't be trusted, and we should go back to where we came from. I wasn't angry at her, I was more angry at the people around us. Opposite was a busy pub where people were laughing, and people were pulling up in their cars to record what was happening on their phones. Eventually, a heavily pregnant Lithuanian woman with broken English came out and helped us, not the perfectly healthy, English-speaking men who were just watching. I make the point about English-speaking, because this woman had 10x the bravery to stop a physical fight whilst being pregnant than all the cowards that had their hands in their pockets. Again, I was disheartened and had begun to lose faith in humanity.

A few weeks later, I was verbally abused by a man in my local shop who claimed that I was oppressed, and 'my book' taught me to be a terrorist. I was ignored so much to the point that when I asked the store manager for help, he responded with 'you can take this outside, I don't want any trouble in here'. I wanted the ground to open up and swallow me whole.

At this point, I experienced agoraphobia, PTSD with night terrors; triggers included news articles of similar attacks or anyone who looked like these people, and depression with voices that told me I was not worth helping which is why no one stood up for me, and I was the one to blame for what happened because I was too different. Not only did this affect me, but my family were on edge about all the women's whereabouts at all times, and who was next?

I was without education and work for a long time, and even now I still find myself hesitating when going into new places or accepting new opportunities with the fear of 'What other types of islamophobia could I face?'. 5 years later, and the effects of these attacks still stay with me. I'm vigilant whenever I'm out, making sure I know the time and exact location of where I am, making a mental note of people's height, what they are wearing, eye colour, and registration numbers in case something does happen. It is exhausting. However, I'm in a much better place than where I was 5 years ago, and I can actively respond in the face of hate with goodness and love.

It is with a heavy heart that I no longer wear the niqab around Norfolk or when I am on my own as Islamophobia has increased, however I still wear it proudly when I am travelling, at events or when public speaking. I'm still raising awareness and, if anything, these events have fuelled my drive to continue with my mission.

Please bear in mind, this is just scratching the surface of what I have experienced as I have not mentioned the daily hate myself and other Muslims face, and there are many other women and men who have experienced far worse on a greater level of hate and violence. I'm very grateful and blessed to not be a victim of any other form of terrorism such as acid throwing, gun and knife crime, or vehicle violence. I'm also grateful to have recovered from my eating difficulties and become a more content version of me as well as growing every day...but experiencing mental distress is harrowing and I wish nothing but peace for those in distress.

You can find out more about where I work here: **www.inspiritedminds.org.uk** and you can find me ranting daily on Instagram: **minha_of_norwich**

Meanha's raw poem gives us a peek at her Warrior power behind her niqab...

My niqab;

It stops me from cutting, smoking and unnecessary hating.

It stops me from doubting, tripping and unnecessary sinning.

It stops me from greed, so I take heed and therefore I am freed.

My niqab;

It reignites hoping, helping and necessary loving.

It's rejuvenating, enlightening and absolutely voicing.

It is my own deed, that I desperately need and therefore I am freed.

My niqab;

A veil of honour, a piece of Armor

Protecting a wild flower that holds superpower

Strong enough for a stampede, promised to succeed, and therefore I am freed.

My niqab;

What is it that you see? Oppression to a certain degree? Would it be crazy, to say that, the thing that oppresses me is the very thing that sets me free?

My niqab;

It's more than just modesty, beyond bodily, above policy, and in all honesty, I'm saying this politely, this is no apology.

For I am a woman that is no wannabe, I refuse to play this monopoly of terrorism and sexism, feminism and fascism.

I am not to be used as a euphemism.

This dogmatism is part of a larger mechanism, but I do not participate in this escapism.

Why?

My niqab;

My identity that I have been beaten for, spat at and ashamed.

Yes, I have pained, but I will not be trained to be chained to the ideals of this society.

Based on vanity, silently, unjustifiably causing anxieties.

For I am a woman of La Ilaha Illa Allah, a statement that is engraved, and allows me to be unscathed.

Once a 'victim' to her scars, inspirational Sylvia is now a proud campaigner for body acceptance

As Sylvia says; You can't change what happens to you in life, but you can change the way you walk forwards on your path. After years of depression and not feeling good enough due to a horrendous accident when she was a child, one day Sylvia decided to '#Emerge Proud' from behind her cloak of protection, and shine like the star that she was meant to be!

At the age of 3, I was hospitalized from an accident

at home falling into boiling water. After surviving life support, I went on to have numerous surgical procedures and operations. Every aspect of growing up in a society with a so called 'perfect body image' left me screaming inside. No matter how much support I received from family members, I could never love or appreciate my body and all the pain it was going through.

When I hit my teens, one thing that stood out to me was body image and looking beautiful. My school friends spent most of their time grooming themselves in front of the mirror and then there was the glossy magazines with flawless images. I recall hearing my mother's friends say 'thank God it's not on her face', but I converted those words to 'the scars on her body are ugly and she is too'.

The hospital consultants continually told my mother that I should stay covered up from the sun and, as most burn victim or survivors know, that this is all year round. Those words certainly had an effect on the rest of my life. Then there were all the hospital visits where my scarring was examined by student doctors. The only problem for me was that uncovering in front of a bunch of strangers really took its toll on my mental health.

As I went into adulthood, I found myself feeling more and more anxious, often suffering panic attacks, believing that everyone knew I was burned. As a burn victim, I found myself attracting undesirables who would take my insecurities for granted, so I allowed myself to be abused both physically, sexually and mentally. I finally hit rock bottom, drinking copious amounts of alcohol daily. And then I met someone who fell in love with me and didn't worry about my scars. We went on to have children together - but no amount of love was going to undo years of self-hate. I began drinking heavily and often turning up at my children's school intoxicated. Each day was different for me, where I would either be happy and attacking everyone, then the next day thinking of how I could end it all.

I found myself trapped in a bubble of self-conscious thoughts and low self-esteem, lacking confidence in everything from school, work, relationships and society. In 2016 my grandson was born, but I was still locking myself in my bedroom and crying every day. My GP asked that I try counselling but unfortunately it didn't work for me. I began to research severe disfigurement on the body but each time I was presented with 'facial disfigurement'. I couldn't understand why, when I almost lost my life twice and suffered 3rd/4th degree burns to my body, it wasn't being acknowledged. I understood how difficult it was for a person with facial difference to deal with this every day, but I also knew that I was suffering too. My mental health was severely affected as well as dealing with lifelong physical pain.

In summer 2016, I was on holiday with my mother and noticed someone filming me. I dropped my sarong off my shoulders and my scarring was on display. We left the pool for the beach where my mother asked questions about my scars and I realised that she could have suffered PTSD, Guilt and so much more. I took this moment to help change her life by strutting to the water's edge and uncovering my scars.

This was the beginning of my Love Disfigure journey to body acceptance and helping support others online come to terms with their visible or hidden differences. I shared an online video-reveal and spoke about what I had endured throughout my life. I set up a Facebook group to encourage people who look different, both facially and/or BODILY, to embrace the way they look. I didn't want anyone to go through years of depression and suicidal thoughts as I had done.

It wasn't long until I received worldwide messages, and I was quickly changing other people's lives through my campaigning. I was even more surprised to hear from people who had all types of struggles including bipolar, depression and even stretch marks who wanted to become involved.

Now is the time for us all to become more diverse and inclusive in this body-obsessed society that we live in through educating and campaigning. It might have taken a lifetime to get here but it's all been worth it helping others to accept the way they look. I now campaign for more diversity within the fashion industry, TV & film industry and, above all, within society. We are all survivors and should be proud of our bodies and how amazing they are regardless of how they look. The more we talk about how we feel through our own real-life stories, the more awareness is raised so that our children can grow up in a world of body-acceptance and true diversity.

Always accept a compliment

You won't be able to change your path in life but you can change the way you walk it

We totally agree with you Sylvia!

Follow Sylvia's inspirational work here:

https://www.lovedisfigure.com/

Instagram – love_disfigure

Twitter – LoveDisfigure

FB Group – LOVE DISFIGURE

"Inside all of us is the power to change the world"

— Roald Dahl

Resources for Experiencers

Helplines and Crisis support:

UK

BEAT: 0808 801 0677 / Youthline: 0808 801 0711

Weight Matters: 020 7622 7727

Eating Disorders Association: 0300 123 3355

Anorexia and Bulimia Care: 0300 011 1213

The Mix (Under 25s) Helpline: 0808 808 4994

MGEDT (Men Get Eating Disorders Too):
http://mengetedstoo.co.uk/

National Eating Disorders Association:
https://www.nationaleatingdisorders.org

International

International Eating Disorder organisation
https://www.eatingdisorderhope.com/treatment-for-eating-disorders/international

Mirror Mirror: *http://www.mirror-mirror.org/*

F.E.A.S.T. (Families Empowered and Supporting
Treatment of Eating Disorders)
https://www.feast-ed.org

USA

NEDA (National Eating Disorders Association) :
http://www.nationaleatingdisorders.org/

Helpline: 1-800-931-2237

T-Feed (Trans Folx Fighting Eating Disorders):
http://www.transfolxfightingeds.org/

N.A.M.E.D. (The National Association for Males
with Eating Disorders): *http://namedinc.org/*

Australia

The Butterfly Foundation for Eating Disorders:
http://thebutterflyfoundation.org.au/

Helpline: 1800334673

NEDC (National Eating Disorders Collaboration):
http://www.nedc.com.au/

Aligned organisations / therapists:

SoulShine: *http://soul-shine.org.uk*

BEAT: *https://www.beateatingdisorders.org.uk*

A Disorder for Everyone:
http://www.adisorder4everyone.com

Body Dysmorphic Disorder Foundation:
https://bddfoundation.org

Compassionate Mental Health:
http://compassionatementalhealth.co.uk

Inner Compass: moving away from diagnosis /
coming off medication support:
https://www.theinnercompass.org

Hub of Hope: *https://hubofhope.co.uk*

Chasing the Stigma:
https://chasingthestigma.co.uk/hub-of-hope/

The Body Positive.org:
https://www.thebodypositive.org

Wednesday's Child:
https://wednesdayschild.co.uk/pages/who-why

Love Disfigure: *https://www.lovedisfigure.com/*

Somatic Coaching:
https://www.elliepaskell.com/somaticcoaching

Changing Faces:
https://www.changingfaces.org.uk/about-us

Body positive yoga: *https://bodypositiveyoga.com*

Katie Piper Foundation (Burns and Scars):
https://katiepiperfoundation.org.uk/#

Peter Breggin: *https://breggin.com*

Brene Brown: *https://brenebrown.com*

Beyond Meds: *https://beyondmeds.com*

Kelly Brogan MD: *kellybroganmd.com/*

Recommended Reading / Viewing

Books:

Body Positive Power by Megan Jayne Crabbe aka @ BodyPosiPanda

Nourishing Wisdom by Marc David

The Gift of our Compulsions by Mary O'Malley

The Body is not an apology by Sonya Renee Taylor

Health at Every Size© by Dr. Linda Bacon

The Gifts of Imperfection by Dr. Brene Brown

What a time to be alone by Chidera Eggerue

The body image blueprint by Jenny Eden Berk, MSEd

Eating in the light of the moon by Dr. Anita Johnston

Grain brain by Dr Perlmutter

Unbearable Weight by Susan Bordo

Fat is a Feminist Issue by Susie Orbach

Brain over Binge by Kathryn Hansen

Intuitive Eating by Evelyn Tribole

Healing your hungry heart by Joanne Poppink MFT

Hunger, A memoir of (my) body by Roxane Gay

Films:

Embrace by Taryn Brumfitt

The Illusionists: https://theillusionists.org/hello/

Heal: http://www.healdocumentary.com

I am Maris

The Call to Courage, Brene Brown

Social Media:

Twitter:
@soulshineyou
@theslumflower #saggyboobsmatter movement
@bodyposipanda
@sonyareneetaylor
@isitpretty
@scarrednotscared
@sitting_pretty
@bopo.boy
@i_weigh
@fatandfab88
@bodykindfestival

Facebook:
"Embrace" Yourself & Your Body With SoulShine
https://www.facebook.com/soulshinehealingAmy/

PODCASTS:

Peace Within Radio including SoulShine's Podcast
Russell Brand - Under the Skin
Fearne Cotton - Happy Place

**The resources in the above lists are taken from those
indicated as helpful by the #EmergingProud and
SoulShine communities when consulted specifically for
this project. They are examples and by no means meant
as an exclusive or exhaustive list.*

Self Care Tips from Amy

"Your Body is not your masterpiece. It's the paintbrush you use to create your masterpiece"
Glennon Doyle

In an appearance-obsessed world, being kind to yourself and your body is a rebellious act. In a world that is determined to keep you small, taking up space is a revolution.

The stories held in this book have hopefully inspired you to see yourself with new eyes and helped you appreciate not only your body but your whole self. Understanding that there is so much more to you than your appearance, the magic that is YOU goes way beyond your physicality.

You are not here to be attractive, you do not owe the world pretty... you are here to do AMAZING things.

Some recommended Self-Care tips:

1. **Embodying practices:** Sometimes, our mental chatter can be overbearing and make us feel heavy and overwhelmed. Embodying practices, such as humming, singing, chanting, dancing, yoga, meditating and BREATHING, not only bring us into the present moment, but allow us to relish in the delightful feeling of being Alive. This gives us a chance to create space between thoughts, by becoming Embodied and re-

connecting with how our body FEELS instead of scrutinizing it for how it looks.

2. **Move in a way that feels GOOD for you,** setting the intention to take focus away from how much fat and calories you will burn to honing in on how Amazing you feel doing the movement. When do you feel most Free and Alive? I feel my most freest and my most true self when I am dancing around to my favourite music.

3. **Create a sacred space,** be it an altar where you keep things that are meaningful to you, or a room that is your safe haven and your chance to reconnect with yourself.

4. **Spend time in nature,** whether it's by the sea, a woodland or even just some fresh air outside your house or your office, spending time in the natural world not only brings us freedom but can reconnect us to our presence, our aliveness. If you witness the natural world, you won't notice any trees beating themselves up over how they look or how they could be better... trees are beautifully rooted in the ground and reach high up in the sky. They are just being them and all the trees work beneath the surface to support and nourish one another. We could learn so much from them.

5. **Practice Gratitude.** Take a moment to look at all the blessings you have in your life. Everything that has happened has brought you to this

moment and has made you the person you are today. Be grateful for the smallest of things, maybe things you take for granted. Be grateful for your bed? Maybe that you have a roof over your head? Maybe you have access to food and clean water? Maybe you have someone who really cares for you? Maybe you are grateful to wake up every day? Starting small and working up, inviting more gratitude into your life can transform the way you see and show up in life.

6. **Build up your inner wellspring of self worth**
Whether it be writing down an affirmation and sticking it to your bathroom mirror, creating an empowering and uplifting mantra to chant to yourself every morning, surrounding yourself with people who remind you of your innate worthiness, smiling at yourself when you catch your reflection, listening to uplifting music that makes you feel powerful and ready to take on the world, becoming aware of those inner critics that try to keep you small... whatever it may be, create a life that reflects your innate worthiness back to you. Your self-worth does NOT depend on how well your jeans fit, it doesn't depend on how much you please other people...it is innately yours and it is already within you.

7. **You are SO much more than your appearance.**
Let's take a moment to focus on your gifts and your traits that don't involve your physical body. Think of someone you love and admire, what are their qualities? Maybe they are kind, considerate,

brave, artistic, creative, active, funny, playful, loving... if you are recognising it in someone else that means you have that potential within you too. If you spot it, you got it!

8. **Become aware of what's energising you** and what is draining you. Say YES to the things that energise and nurture you and NO to the things that drain your energy or no longer serve you. Set boundaries! This is easier said than done sometimes: I highly recommend Braving the Wilderness by Brené Brown for guidance on setting healthy boundaries.

9. **Thank Your Body** for all the things it does for you every second of every day. While you are reading this, your heart is pumping, your lungs are breathing, your digestive system is working to turn the food you ate earlier into energy, your cells are being healed and renewed. There are thousands of biochemical reactions happening that we have no say in, our body does that on its own. Let's thank it for what it does and allows us to do instead of criticising it for not looking how we think we 'should' look.

10. **Read.** Take a look at our recommended reading list in the Resources section of this book for some empowering and life-changing reading.

11. **Create with your heart.** Creativity can come in as many different forms as there are people in this world, whether it's writing, dancing, painting,

sculpting, singing... tap into those creative juices running through you. Try focusing on the process of creating as opposed to the end product...get messy, have a play and tap into your inner child.

12. **Trust the healing process.** The road to recovery is not always a linear one, sometimes it's a case of taking one step forward and two steps back and that's ok.

13. **Connect with supportive and inspiring people,** who are willing to listen without judgement and an open heart.

14. **Find a safe space** to be vulnerable, to speak your truth, express your feelings. Maybe with a therapist or a mentor.

15. **Join a support group.** Connect with people who are going through similar things and build each other up.

16. **Take control over what you see in the media** and what you allow to infiltrate your consciousness. This means: throwing out any magazines or books that seem to shame other people's bodies. This means: having a social media detox from people who are posting unrealistic images, selling harmful diet culture 'quick fix' products. This means: watching uplifting documentaries that leave you feeling inspired and excited about life, instead of diminishing you and making you feel inadequate.

17. **Diversify your social media feed.** All day, every day we are bombarded with images from different kinds of screens. Much of the time, images that have been edited and tampered with. Taking control of what we are seeing can drastically improve our mental health and wellbeing. Choosing to see more body diversity and venturing out of the mainstream media will not only allow your brain to create new neural pathways and create a new 'normal', but you will feel more uplifted and at peace with yourself. I would highly recommend filling your feed with authentic and inspiring people such as: @bodyposipanda @bopo.boy @scarrednotscared

18. **Celebrate every success.** Sometimes all these things can seem too much or even unimaginable to do. Sometimes self-care comes in the form of getting out of bed in the morning, cleaning your teeth, having a wash...Give yourself a pat on the back and celebrate every success you can. You are doing an amazing job and we are so proud of you for not giving up...

You can do this!

Tips to keep yourself safe:

- Remember that your thoughts do not have to take charge - you can have them without acting on them

- If you are feeling like hurting yourself, wait, even if it's for 5 minutes, but just wait, and... breathe...This may be hard but it's likely the intensity will subside

- Call a person or group you can trust to open up to about how you feel

- Find a safe way to express any emotions that are surfacing

- Call a helpline

"True belonging is the spiritual practice of believing in and belonging to yourself so deeply that you can share your most authentic self with the world and find sacredness in both being a part of something and standing alone in the wilderness. True belonging doesn't require you to change who you are; it requires you to be who you are."

— Brené Brown

Acknowledgements

My infinite thanks go to the incredible Kinda Proud team; the book Reps, and especially Amy Woods for spearheading, and Mandy Horne for editing, this particular edition in the series, our Publisher Sean Patrick of *That Guy's House* and PR Consultant Jenna Owen of *Media Jems*, all of whom have passionately and without question donated their time and expertise in order to support this project to fruition. It's a vision we all share, and one that would not have been possible to achieve without each and every one of us coming together with no agenda other than wanting to disseminate hope like confetti around the world...

The team also extends our immense gratitude to everyone in this pocket book, who have bravely gifted their personal transformation story with the hope that it helps at least one other person in the world to find their own inner spark to initiate or aid their recovery journey. We aim for these books to create a 'positive domino effect', rippling out HOPE to those who need it most.

Our gratitude also goes to The Missing Kind charity who seed-funded this project as an official Sponsor.

Without all of these team players there would be no HOPE confetti, so together we celebrate the incredible power of heart-founded collaboration, and a shared vision and mission.

The Kinda Proud Team

Other titles in our Kinda Proud Pocket Books of Hope and Transformation series so far:

#Emerging Proud through NOTEs
(non ordinary transcendent experiences)

#Emerging Proud through Suicide

#Emerging Proud through Trauma and Abuse

Hope

It's all I need

to lift my heart

out of the depths

and into the light

— Ambriel